THE
ROYAL PATH
OF SHAKTI

"The illuminating visualizations give readers a viable spiritual path to face and overcome disease, difficulties, and even death and to truly taste the amrita of the Kaulas. This wondrous book is a sacred invitation into divine embodiment of the Kaula yogini mysteries of the cosmos. A must-read and invaluable guide of never-before-revealed ancient yogini wisdom."

LAURA K. AMAZZONE, AUTHOR OF
GODDESS DURGĀ AND SACRED FEMALE POWER

THE
ROYAL PATH
OF SHAKTI

The Erotic and
Magical Techniques of
Kaula Tantra

Daniel Odier

Translated by Jack Cain

Inner Traditions
Rochester, Vermont

Inner Traditions
One Park Street
Rochester, Vermont 05767
www.InnerTraditions.com

Text stock is SFI certified

Copyright © 2022 by Daniel Odier and Éditions Almora
English translation copyright © 2023 by Inner Traditions International

Originally published in French in 2022 under the title *Kaula: la voie royale de la Shakti* by Éditions Almora, Paris
First U.S. edition published in 2023 by Inner Traditions

Cataloging-in-Publication Data for this title is available from the Library of Congress

ISBN 978-1-64411-716-3 (print)
ISBN 978-1-64411-717-0 (ebook)

Printed and bound in the United States by Lake Book Manufacturing, LLC
The text stock is SFI certified. The Sustainable Forestry Initiative® program promotes sustainable forest management.

10 9 8 7 6 5 4 3 2 1

Text design and layout by Priscilla Harris Baker
This book was typeset in Garamond Premier Pro with Ancient Zurich, Fritz Quadrata, Hypatia, Laureate, and Majesty used as display typefaces

To send correspondence to the author of this book, mail a first-class letter to the author c/o Inner Traditions • Bear & Company, One Park Street, Rochester, VT 05767, and we will forward the communication, or contact the author directly at **www.danielodier.com**.

In a word, the way of liberation resides in the
Kula Dharma, the Royal Path of Shakti.

KULARNAVA TANTRA

Contents

PART II

The *Kaulajnananirnaya Tantra*

Preface

$\mathcal{T}$he *Kaulajnananirnaya Tantra* of Mahasiddha Matsyendranath is the pivotal tantra that marks the transition from the magic and erotic tradition of Assam to the refined philosophical tradition of the great Kashmiri masters Somananda, Abhinavagupta, Kallata, and Utpaladeva, spanning the period from the ninth and tenth centuries up to the poetical flowering of Lalla in the fourteenth century.

The arrival of Matsyendranath in Kashmir and Nepal and the transmission of the Kaula Way, the Path of Shakti, are considered fundamental by Abhinavagupta. He pays homage to the Mahasiddha in the first chapter of his monumental *Tantraloka,** where he writes: "May Matsyendranath be auspicious for me. It is he who cast the net, the net steeped in red, crisscrossed with knots and gaps, that extends and stretches to all locations."†

What is notable in the *Kaulajnananirnaya Tantra* is that he also points out a connection, a continuation with the ancient Shaivism of the Indus Valley. This connection is the preeminence of the yoginis and of respect for the feminine in all its forms— whether it be human, vegetable, or animal, such respect being

---

*Abhinavagupta, *Luce delle sacre scritture (Tantrāloka),* ed. Raniero Gnoli Turin: Unione Tipografico-editrice Torinese, 1972.
†"Steeped in red" refers to the "Shakti net" that Matsyendranath weaves in order to capture the giant fish that has just swallowed his text.

essential to the wish for union with all that is. Matsyendranath could be an answer to the mystery of the transmission of teachings between the disappearance of civilization from the Indus Valley 1,700 years before our era and the resurgence of the teachings in Kashmir at the beginning of our era.

In the *Kaulajnana** we find all the magic practices connected with obtaining *siddhis* (magical powers), such as the ability to hear at great distances, to be present in several places at the same time, to travel great distances in a few moments, to penetrate through solid matter, and to defend oneself from enemies. Such powers also included black magic practices such as enslaving, destroying, or paralyzing. More surprising, and rarely mentioned among the siddhis by other sources, is obtaining the gift of poetry and experiencing the freeing power of the word.

Matsyendranath lived with his consort Konkanamba, the mother of Konka, at Kamarupa, a sacred site that mythology tells us was the place where Shakti's yoni fell when she was dismembered by Vishnu. Konkanamba was considered a Mahasiddha. She and Matsyendranath were incarnations of the magic Shiva-Shakti couple and together they taught the practices of the Kaula Way, which would have been lost if it had not been transmitted by Lalita Devi's lineage. Their text just barely touches on this topic without embarking on the transmission of the actual practices. They were revered as Kuleshvara and Kuleshvari.† Matsyendranath and Konkanamba traveled to Kashmir, taking the route through Nepal. They established the Kaula tradition by creating several practice centers in locations between Assam and Kashmir. Matsyendranath died on one of these trips, at Patan, where he lived in a temple that still exists today, as does a column erected there in his memory. He and his companion

---

*Abbreviation of *Kaulajnananirnaya.*

†Kuleshvara and Kuleshvari are male and female incarnations or idealized representations of the Kaula (or Kula) Way.

lived four generations before Abhinavagupta (950–1020). The Kaula lineage proceeding on from them was as follows: Matsyendranath and Konkanamba transmitted to several disciples, of whom nine were their own children. One of the children transmitted the teaching to Sumati, who transmitted it to Somadeva, and finally it was transmitted to Ambunatha, who was Abhinavagupta's master.

In the *Sahasranamam*, which contains the thousand names of Shri Lalita Devi, a manifestation of Durga, we find a connection to the Kaula Way: "O Thou, divinity in the Kula sphere, I pay homage to Thee. O Thou, whom the adepts of the Kaula tradition venerate, I pay homage to Thee" (sts. 440–41).

In the *Kaulajnana* there is a brief autobiographical passage on Matsyendranath containing underpinnings of legendary magic:

When you (Devi) and I were going to Candradvipa (the Island of the Moon), we were joined by Vatuka Karttikeya. Even though he was ignorant, I entrusted this Shastra to him. O Devi! The instruction given to Skanda was in vain: he stole the knowledge and threw it into the sea. Bhadre! So I went to the ocean and after having caught the fish that had swallowed the Shastra, I made an incision to open its stomach. After having recovered the books of knowledge from the fish's stomach, I hid them in a secret location. Once more, Kruddha adopted the appearance of a mouse and stole them in order to throw them into the ocean. Once again, they were gobbled up by a fish of immeasurable size! Furious, I made a Shakti net. I caught this fish, which was submerged in seven seas. However, this fish was as strong as I was. Because of his spiritual strength, he was difficult to vanquish even for the thirty-three gods. Giving up my position as a Brahmin, I became a fisherman and I caught the fish with my Shakti net. By making a gash to open him, the Kulagama* was recovered once again. Even though

---

*Another way of saying the "Kaula Way."

*I was a Brahmin, O Supreme One, I acted as a fisherman. Since the Brahmin rescued the knowledge from the stomach of the fish by killing it, he was known as Matsyaghna.** Because the Lord of the Brahmins acted as a fisherman, he became Kaivarta (the fisherman).* (Patala 16)

The twenty-four chapters (*patalas*) of the *Kaulajnana* broach the following topics:

1. From the tips of the big toes emanate the *tattvas*.
2. Fire kicks off dissolution.
3. Kaula characteristics: the senses, the object of the senses, and the body are Shakti.
4. Intense practice and opening the *nadis*.
5. Alchemical knowledge, the light of the moon.
6. Where Shiva resides in the body, *amrita* or sublime essence.
7. The chakras nourished by lunar light.
8. The *sadhana* of the sixty-four yoginis.
9. *Siddhas,* mantras, molten gold flowing through the chakras.
10. The round of Sanskrit letters in the body.
11. Feeding, the sacred substances of Shakti.
12. The Way is to act according to one's own will.
13. Inner repetition of the *Hamsa* mantra.
14. The eight *siddhis,* the heart center, the beautiful perspiration of lunar milk. Shakti.
15. The Sahaja chakra.
16. The siddhi yoginis, sexual union. Autobiographical fragments. Vatuka.
17. The vital breath, the central channel, Shiva-Shakti unity. Neither meditation nor non-meditation.

---

*[*Matsyaghna* means "killer of fish" in Sanskrit. —*Trans.*]

18. The worship of the siddhas, the yoginis, and the guru.
19. The worship of the black yoginis and the siddhi yoginis.
20. The path of sexual love. The *vira* (hero) and his Shakti.
21. The various Kaula paths.
22. The hidden *lingam* and the worship of the guru.
23. The animal, vegetable, and human forms of the Kaula yoginis.
24. The red yoginis.

The *Kaulajnana* is above all a text on practice and, like many other tantras, it is written in a "twilight" language, meaning a text that outlines the practice without revealing its esoteric aspects, which are to be received by transmission from one's master. Lalita Devi took great care to explain each practice to me, and to have me discover everything that was not written explicitly in the text. The *Kaulajnana* is actually a kind of crib sheet or reminder list that names the practice without saying how it begins or how it ends. Without further explanation, it is therefore impossible to conduct these practices. That is why I have chosen to separate them and describe them in detail before giving the full text of Dominique Boubouleix's magnificent work, which to my knowledge is the first French version of this text translated directly from Sanskrit. What I am writing here is the third installment of the teachings of Lalita Devi, following my books *Tantric Quest: An Encounter with Absolute Love** and *Crazy Wisdom of the Yogini: Teachings of the Kashmiri Mahamudra Tradition.*[†]

Without preludes and postludes, the textual rendering of the practices is not savored in the same way. What is missing is the night-blue space, how to begin, the way the visualization appears, and the conclusion: generally a return to the body that has undergone an

---

*Rochester, Vt.: Inner Traditions, 1997.
†Rochester, Vt.: Inner Traditions, 2021.

alchemical transmutation and has found once again the memory of infinite space. Here is an example:

> Let us meditate on the image of an eight-petalled chakra, colored white like the Moon and located where the spine meets the skull, that is, where one's hairline begins. We can gratify our bodies thanks to this light. (Patala 7)

And here is the complete practice as taught by Lalita:

You are floating naked, seated in night-blue space. Your breathing is becoming more and more finely subtle. It transforms into a breathing cycle that forms an energy loop moving across your palate, descending along the central channel, looping around the perineum and coming back up in front of the spine. Behind you a magnificent full moon appears. You feel its rays shining on your skin, but you cannot see it. Your desire to rest your gaze upon it is so great that you imagine that your eyes turn back slowly and focus on the spot of the secret chakra found in the occiput, where your hairline begins. With your finger, you can feel a slight hollow there. A triangle is formed joining your left eye, your right eye, and the secret chakra that will gradually open so you can see the moon. You gaze at it until the moment when a river of lunar milk emerges from the moon, enters your secret chakra, nourishing the eight-petalled lotus and spreading out impetuously through your head, irrigating your brain with a milky whiteness and carrying away all the dark shadows of suffering, memories, and patterns of conditioning. The tumultuous flow descends through your body, moving through the bones, muscles, organs, nerves, and tendons, carrying with it all traces of darkness. The river of milky light revolves in your pelvic area, touching all parts and moving out into night-blue space continuously until you become nothing but lunar light. Stay in this space until the lunar river ceases to enter you. The secret chakra that opened now closes. Your eyes return to where they belong. The river leaves your body. Be aware of your luminous spatiality and gently come back to where you are, slowly opening your eyes.

Two characteristics of the Kali Yuga are that, during this period of cosmic chaos, secrets must be revealed and practitioners have a greater capacity to integrate them. These positive aspects of this dark period are often ignored by the commentators. Matsyendranath begins his tantra by saying: "What has been kept secret is now revealed" (Patala 1). The Tantra of Great Liberation, the *Mahanirvana Tantra,* also says: "Once the age of Kali is advanced, the Kaula Way will be revealed."* The publication of this tantra is happening then at the designated moment and offers us the deepest practice of the Kaula Way. These practices have a power that has never been fully plumbed, and they are still today luminously wrapped with yogini magic.

The manuscript of the *Kaulajnananirnaya Tantra* was discovered in 1922 in the royal library of Nepal by Prabodh Chandra Bagchi. It was published in 1934, and translated into English by Michael Magee in 1986.† Dominique Boubouleix translated it directly from Sanskrit into French in 1999; it is his unpublished version that I am presenting here, now translated into English.

Tantra of the Great Liberation (Mahānirvāna Tantra), trans. Arthur Avalon [John Woodroffe] (London: Luzac, 1913).
†*Kaulajnana-Nirnaya of the School of Matsyendranatha,* ed. P. C. Bagchi, trans. Michael Magee (Varanasi: Prachya Prakashan, 1986).

There is also a beautiful English version translated by Saktari Mukhopadhyaya and Stella Dupuis.* Magee presents the Sanskrit text; Dupuis presents the text in Devanagari and Sanskrit.

In order to facilitate the ease of reading, but above all to re-create the direct and subtle perfume of Lalita Devi's transmission, mouth to mouth, as it is said in the *Kaulajnananirnaya Tantra* and the *Kularnava Tantra,*† I have decided not to use diacritics since they don't influence the pronunciation for someone who doesn't know Sanskrit. I have also dropped brackets and most parentheses since they make the text difficult to read. In this way, the taste of the oral teaching is retained in authentic vibration for those parts of the text that concern the practices. I have also chosen to directly insert the translation of certain Sanskrit words in order to avoid endlessly breaking up the reading with a link to notes or a glossary. Finally, I have not commented on certain explicit practices in the text.

In the second part of the book, you will find the complete Dominique Boubouleix version of the text (here translated into English). I thank him for having entrusted me with this text, which immediately resonated with Lalita's teaching and which allowed me to recognize all the passages that she referred to in her teaching. For her, Matsyendranath was the carrier of the whole yogini lineage that she was proud to belong to. Lalita owned no books. She knew the main texts and a great many of the poems by heart. She was a yogini and not a scholar. She loved to go to

---

The Kaulajñānanirṇaya: The Esoteric Teachings of Matsyendrapāda, Sadguru of the Yoginī Kaula School in the Tantra Tradition, edited and translated by Satkari Mukhopadhyaya with Stella Dupuis (New Delhi: Aditya Prakashan, 2012).

†In order to understand this type of transmission, see the description of Lalita's teaching in my book *Crazy Wisdom of the Yogini: Teachings of the Kashmiri Mahamudra Tradition,* trans. Jack Cain (Rochester, Vt.: Inner Traditions, 2021).

the heart of things without making precise references. Each time that I asked her where something was in the *Kaulajnananirnaya Tantra,* she would smile and reply: "I am placing it in your heart and that will be your library. Knowledge is not practice and Matsyendranath took care to conceal the practice so that only he who had received the direct transmission could penetrate the mysteries of the twilight language."

PART I

Practices

The Emergence of Tattvas

From the tips of the big toes emanate the tattvas.

PATALA 1

"*T*he tantrika must be pure of heart, supremely joyful, devoid of anger and turning thought. He rejects inferior ritual. He is warmhearted and worships the lineage of the masters. He is generous and full of devotion. He is supported by the lineage of yoginis. He practices formless meditation, *samadhi*."

There are three forms of initiation: by touch, by voice, by the mind. They are without any definite form, without ritual.

The disciple receives the grace of understanding from Shakti's impact.

The body itself is the temple in the Kaula tradition. It harbors the thirty-six tattvas, or the thirty-six categories, stretching from the five basic elements up to the absolute, which is beyond Shiva/Shakti. It is therefore not necessary to deny the body or abandon it in order to know union with the divine, but, on the contrary, to liquefy it, to make it like earth, water, fire, air, and ether. Practice awakens the body and makes it vibrate (*spanda*). The body becomes aware that it is the cosmos.

The thirty-six tattvas and the absolute tattva that crowns them:

THE FIVE ELEMENTS

- Earth
- Water
- Fire
- Air
- Ether

THE FIVE ELEMENTS OF SENSE

- Smell
- Taste
- Form
- Touch
- Sound

THE FIVE ORGANS OF ACTION

- Creation
- Excretion
- Foot
- Hand
- Speech

THE FIVE ORGANS OF PERCEPTION

- Nose
- Tongue
- Eye
- Skin
- Ear

THE FIVE INTERNAL ORGANS

- Mind
- Intellect
- Ego (linked to objectivity)
- Nature
- Ego (linked to subjectivity)

THE SIX PROTECTIVE SHELLS

- Limitation of space
- Limitation of time
- Limitation of attachment
- Limitation of knowledge
- Limitation of creativity
- Illusion of individuality

THE FIVE SUBTLE ELEMENTS

- Subjectivity invested with power in action
- Awareness of one's own absolute nature
- The universal Self
- Shakti
- Shiva

THE ABSOLUTE

- Beyond Shiva/Shakti*

---

*For a detailed description of the tattvas, see Lalita Devi's teaching in my books *Tantric Quest: An Encounter with Absolute Love,* trans. Jody Gladding (Rochester, Vt.: Inner Traditions, 1997), and *Tantra, la dimension sacrée de l'érotisme.*

PRACTICE 2

The Body on Fire

The fire known as Kalagnirudra is eternally situated in the tip of the nail of the big toe. When it flames upward, then dissolution is set in motion.

PATALA 2

This practice is also found in two stanzas of the *Vijnanabhairava Tantra:* "Concentrate on the fire raging more and more as it rises up from your feet and completely consumes you. When all that is left is ashes scattered by the wind, know the tranquility of space that returns to space." And: "See the entire world transformed into a gigantic firestorm. Then, when nothing is left but ashes, enter into beatitude."*

Ash has always been considered to be a purifier. It also stays very hot when it is applied to the body or when one is buried in an ash pit, as we did with Lalita. It is here that there also begins the practice in night-blue space. You can imagine the Earth seen from space. In the first practice you are consumed and disappear into space; in the second, you direct the fire toward Earth, which bursts into flame, is consumed entirely, and disappears. You then dwell in the spatiality of *samadhi*.

---

*Daniel Odier, trans., *Tantra Yoga: Le Vijñânabhaïrava tantra, Le "tantra de la connaissance supreme"* (Paris: Michel, 2004), 20.

PRACTICE 3

The Five Elements

Where the mind resides, there dwell also the senses, the objects of the senses, and the body—they are impregnated by one's own Shakti, one's embodied being, and the five tattvas.

PATALA 3

*T*his is an essential point of our practice. The body is the cosmos, the body is Shakti. Shakti resides in the first five tattvas: earth, water, fire, wind, and ether. The practice takes place in the integration of the tattvas and the body, which then becomes the sole residence of Shakti.

You float in night-blue space, nude and seated. The yoga of the five elements or tattvas is the beginning of the transformation of the ordinary body into a cosmic body. Through this practice the yogi becomes all that is—the totality.

Earth

Meditate on your body as being a cube of earth floating in night-blue space. Little by little, your body is transformed into liquid gold. It shines in space and conquers illness. After three years of this practice, the body becomes adamantine. It is inhabited by the strength of nine elephants, and it enters into *spanda* (continuous vibration). Breathing stabilizes in the heart. The yogi must see himself as being Shakti. She resides in the heart and illuminates the body with her own radiance seated on a black lotus. The

6

yogi spreads his luminosity across the world and becomes like the tattva of the Earth.

Water

Floating in night-blue space, your body is in the shape of a half moon, a white lotus at your throat. Imagine your body cool like a full moon and submerged in the ocean. Think: *There is nothing else either in me or outside of me. My body liquefies. My seeing becomes like water.* Your body rises up above the water. It conquers illness, becomes water. It is filled with a lunar glow spreading out from the lotus of the throat. It becomes equal to the tattva of water.

Fire

You see your body as a triangle surrounded by a belt of fire. A fire emerges from your body and burns everything outside of you. Illness leaves you. After a season of practice, you can burst what you touch into flames and you can become fire. You enter into vibration. You are the spirit of fire. You view yourself then in your human form. You meditate on your palate, which produces a sparkling fire surrounded with smoke, like the sun in smoke. In this way you become the element fire and you master the mantras. You spread your light across the world and you experience the stillness of Shakti.

Wind

You visualize yourself as a night-blue sphere in which six drops of a lighter blue are floating. The drops vibrate and produce a sound, a celestial music. You free yourself from illness. You are able to go great distances without being tired, and you take the form of the wind. You visualize your night-blue body. It becomes the wind tattva in the form of a sparkling sapphire. You become unable to be seized.

Ether

Your night-blue body clarifies, little by little, until it turns into ether. You sense spatiality, and you become impervious to the venom of serpents. You are freed from illness. You become space and can pass through the elements. You become invisible and you see the earth as being perforated. You can become the emptiness in a dark, rocky cavity. You visualize the ether at your forehead and you see yourself as the moon devoured by an eclipse. You become Shiva, the lord of mantras.

The practice of the five elements transforms the yogi into these elements. It stabilizes the mind, destroys poisons and egoism, and reveals consciousness. It makes it possible to vanquish reality, which is the ultimate level for the yogi. Consider the siddhis, the magic powers, as a dynamic movement toward the infinite instead of an attainment in reality. Of course it happens that in intense practice one or another siddhi will manifest. Don't ascribe any importance to that. Only the siddhi of being gifted poetically is necessary in order to transmit my teaching.

There is another practice of the five tattvas that is part of the secret instructions and must be done only after the first practice has become familiar. It is a practice that will dissipate your violence and aggressivity, by treating this issue from the inside as in the Kali practices. It is important not to sidestep the problem by vainly trying to transform the violence into love or compassion. We're heading straight into the heart of the rage.

You are seated on the top of a mountain that overlooks a valley where you can see a village.

You will place in this village everyone toward whom you feel some animosity.

You imagine them going about their business. Perhaps there's a market, cafés on the open squares, vehicles, people in their gardens. Let your imagination guide you.

Focus on your body, which is embodying the first tattva—the tattva of earth—and with a forceful out-breath, imagine that liquid earth begins flowing from your body through your feet, dragging along the surrounding earth in an immense landslide that gushes over the town carrying away houses, breaking down walls, as human beings disappear in this flow of mud.

Everything is empty and silent. Your body is calm.

The earth element then becomes a little brown sphere floating in space.

You come back to your body, seated calmly on the mountain, and from there you feel that your body is becoming the tattva of water. It liquefies while retaining its form, while the village and its inhabitants reappear, still rather unconcerned.

You breathe in and out more and more deeply, and then with the final breath out you allow the flood to flow out of you, hurtling down the mountain, becoming a tsunami that carries away everything in its path. Imagine all the details right up to the moment when there isn't the slightest trace of the village and its inhabitants.

You continue breathing calmly on the mountaintop.

The water element becomes a little sphere floating in space.

The village reappears gradually with its inhabitants.

Your body then becomes the fire tattva.

You are shot through with live flames coming from your big toes. They rise up in you.

With a great breathing out, you send fire into the valley. The forests burst into flame. The village is reduced to ashes, which spread out into space. Once the cloud is carried away by the winds, nothing is left—only ashes remain.

You come back into your calm body.

The fire element then becomes a little sphere floating in space.
The village reappears.

Your body becomes wind circulating within you.

You let the wind out through all the openings in your body—
a powerful tornado begins to carry away everything in its path.
Trees are flying by, roofs take off, fragile constructions are taken
by a whirlwind in space that swallows everything until the valley
becomes peaceful and empty.

You come back to your body.

The wind element then becomes a little sphere, floating in space.
The village reappears.

You now feel invaded by the ether tattva. It's a much gentler
sensation, as if space were the very stuff of illusion.

The village fades. Everything becomes light, airy, and ends up
being a transparency that eliminates forms and contrasts.

The form of ether then becomes the fifth sphere, floating in
space next to the wind sphere, the fire sphere, the water sphere,
and the earth sphere.

Seeing the five spheres, you disappear as does, in that moment,
all of reality.

All that is left are the five spheres: one earth-colored, one
water-colored, one fire-colored, the wind smoky-colored, and one
the color of the ether or immaterial space.

The earth sphere dissolves into the water sphere.

The water sphere dissolves into the fire sphere.

The fire sphere dissolves into the wind sphere.

The wind sphere dissolves into the ether sphere.

There is nothing left but this impalpable, diaphanous sphere.
Suddenly, it disappears.

PRACTICE 4

The Lingam as Pure Consciousness

Everything manifests from the center of the bindu: Brahma, all the gods and the asuras, the saints, the yakshas, the gandharvas, the siddhas, the plants, the trees, the insects, the planets, the celestial constellations, the stars and all the rest, everything that is found in the cosmos, fixed or in movement, the elements and every other thing. This lingam, the cause of creation and dissolution, is worshipped by the siddhas. It shines with its own light, being pure, eternal, entirely unlimited. It is like the flame at the end of time and like lightning in the sky. One arrives at liberation after having known this vivifying lingam.

PATALA 3

*W*hen you are floating in night-blue space, the lingam becomes both the place of creation and the instrument of creation. It is yoni/lingam. It is the sign of primordial androgyny and of the absolute unity of Shiva/Shakti. In the shape of an oval stone, *salagrama,* it is the union of masculine and feminine. It emerges from the force of Shakti in representations. It is the architecture of the cosmos. Know that the lingam is pure consciousness—eternal, unlimited, and without form. You can visualize yourself as a crystal lingam at the center of space both creator and destructor of all things in the sense that everything becomes space, consciousness, and vibration. So visualize this lingam, which, in an orgasmic flow, creates life in all its forms, a continual springing forth. Or visualize the crystal becoming a lucidity such that it encompasses the whole cosmos.

PRACTICE 5

The Dancing Flames
of the Nadis

Bhairava says: "You do well to ask me that, O Mahadevi.
Therefore, I'm going to speak to you about it. One must
create the Kula of the body by bringing together the apertures
of the nadis, the subtle channels. The pinda consists of a
vidya mantra—the knowledge mantra. It is the splendid
bestower of happiness and liberation. By lighting a flame
above and below the apertures of each nadi, one says 'vam,'
while visualizing these Sanskrit letters being the color of
molten gold. Then, darkness and light will be simultaneously
dissolved in the circle of birth, and the sadhaka (yogi) can
enter the body of the beast he wants. By using 'hum ho,'
he can accomplish that with all fixed and mobile things
simultaneously."

PATALA 4

𝒴ou are floating seated and naked in night-blue space. The very subtle sensation of the nadis cannot come from a concept or an explanation since the sensation depends on the intensity of the practice. Therefore, instead of being the one who practices, which is not yoga, you are going to call upon the flames to instruct you about the sensation of the nadis or subtle channels.

Around your naked and luminous body at the center of

night-blue space, the *"Vam"* mantra sets off the movement of little flames that dance around you. You don't steer them anywhere; you just float, watching them scintillate all around you in a slow, unstructured dance. *"Vam . . . Vam . . . Vam . . ."*

It may happen that the flames come and position themselves at the openings of certain nadis and it may be that they continue their dance if your body isn't open enough. In our yoga, we never force anything—we play with the fire!

PRACTICE 6

Luminous Shakti

In meditating on Shakti as being the Bindu Nada, the drop, the sound, and in bringing together darkness and light to dissolve them in the bursting circle of birth, one must meditate on the fact that such a thing is happening in the body. In half the blink of an eye, anyone can find himself paralyzed. O Magnificent One!

One has to have meditated on Shakti and visualized her as a beautiful woman seated in the five ethers.

PATALA 4

When one meditates on the body of Devi, who exults in an ecstatic love, and when her body is ready for sexual union, she becomes Sahaja Shakti.

The heart of the practice is to feel the cosmos in oneself, to feel Shakti in oneself. This means to have a felt sense of Shakti's body, which exults in an ecstatic love born from the awareness of the totality of her own body. For that, the tantrika must be animated by an incandescent passion. This is one of the points that distinguishes the tantric path from other approaches—passion is at the heart of the dynamic of illumination. Without passion, the body cannot incarnate and receive the totality, personified here by Shakti. Shakti contains the cosmos. Passionate worship makes her enter us. Her ecstatic love takes hold of us. The bindu, the primordial droplet, is creation's sound, the emergence of all forms arising from consciousness.

In night-blue space, you imagine that she is facing you, resplendent. Her erotic energy is that of the whole cosmos. Since for us everything is consciousness and vibration, desire is everywhere. This is what the *Vijnanabhairava Tantra* teaches: "Desire exists in you as it does in all things. Realize that it is found also in objects and in everything that the mind can grasp. Discovering the universality of desire, move into its luminous space."* And Tripura also sings of passion: "Only passion is necessary."†

Shakti becomes more and more luminous. Her connection with the totality is enough to bring her to orgasmic joy. She doesn't need Shiva because Shiva is within her. Observe her androgynous body. One breast, two sets of sexual organs, a moonlike face, an expression in which power and infinite tenderness mix.

The flow of orgasmic pleasure emerges not only from her yoni but also from every pore of her skin in infinite droplets of light that come to rest on your skin. In your breathing, you take nectar into yourself and you become as luminous as she is.

Your body changes. You also become a luminous androgynous being.

The two bodies turn into a luminous halo that dissipates into space.

---

*Odier, trans., *Tantra Yoga,* 27.
†Michel Hulin, trans., *Tripurarahasya, la doctrine secrète de la déesse Tripurā* (Paris: Fayard, 1979).

The Hive

"Hro hrah" attracts the red yoginis.

PATALA 4

*T*his is one of the most mysterious passages in Matsyendranath's tantra. It refers to one of the most beautiful and profound practices, but, as he says at the end of the tantra, sexual practices must be carefully hidden. That is what he is doing here after having said that the secrets must be divulged in the Kali Yuga. The practice is a marvelous way of realizing that the cosmos emanates from the body. In the tantras, bees and the hive are often an allusion to sexual juices.

You are floating in night-blue space. You repeat the *"Hro hrah"* mantra to yourself inwardly in order to attract the red yoginis. However, be careful to always engage in this practice during a moment of great inner stability, otherwise the red yoginis could manifest violently. What's beautiful in this practice is that you will experience two aspects of the red yoginis: their wild aspect and their infinite gentleness. This is a practice that will open the subtle channels of the body. It is more radical than the flame practice, which illuminates the ends of the subtle channels, and it is preferable to start with this one because it makes you aware of the channels. Breathe calmly, stare at infinite space in front of you, and keep on calling the red yoginis. The first one appears suddenly, the size of a bee, in front of your face. She is very beautiful, a fine ruby red, her body is transparent, her smile mischievous. She is animated with a fierce energy and she is vibrating in space. Suddenly, she throws herself at you like a bullet, penetrating your skull, opening a path toward your heart, going through organs as she moves lower in your body and comes out of you at your knee or your foot. As soon as she comes out, she duplicates herself. Two red yoginis come back in front of you and attack again. They penetrate your body violently, opening other channels but always moving through your heart. The process continues at a lively pace—the yoginis doubling each time they come out of you through a different place in your body, 4, 8, 16, 32, 64, 128, and so on, until you are surrounded by a swarm of furious yoginis piercing you everywhere. With this intense circulation, you turn into a vibrating hive. Spanda appears as you begin to take pleasure in this intense circulation. Your whole body is open. Your subtle channels are activated. The red yoginis then manifest the other aspect of their personality. They become very gentle, leaving your body and forming a vibrating protective red sphere around you. There are hundreds of yoginis around you in night-blue space. You feel gentleness and protection. The red yoginis approach gently and each of them lies down in one of the alveoli, just below the skin. You see and you feel that your body is inhabited by the red goddesses from head to toe. They are everywhere at the end of each subtle channel.

Their little bodies undulate gently in you, engendering an intense and refined pleasure. Their movements become more and more sensual, slipping gradually toward climax and reaching orgasm all at the same time. From their yonis there begins to well up a luminous pleasure, white like milk shot through with powdered diamonds. Hundreds of little rivers flow through the subtle channels to your heart, where they join together in a river of light that flows to the center of your body. It's the size of your fist and it moves through your diaphragm, through your organs. For this practice, visualize your body as female. That will allow you, little by little, to integrate the presence of Shiva/Shakti, and to move beyond the limitations that we have when we are only a woman or a man. Feel your uterus, your yoni. The river of light fills you and moves through you. The red yoginis are in orgasmic pleasuring continuously. Hundreds of rivers run through you. You are traversed by the flow.

Suddenly, the river emerges from your yoni into night-blue space. Its light is intense. The flow begins to move off into space in a beautiful arc. Suddenly, it breaks up into thousands of stars and begins to turn into the Milky Way. You are the creator of the cosmos. The Milky Way surrounds you, passing in front of your center, your heart, your breasts, your face. It moves above you and descends, facing your spinal column.

When it passes under you, the red yoginis stop their pleasuring and the river moves out of you completely. At that moment, the river is joined by the Milky Way moving back up.

At the center of night-blue space, you observe the Milky Way and the cosmos.

The red yoginis melt, little by little, within you and their imprint stabilizes in your body.

PRACTICE 8

The Garland of Letters

By separating out each bija from the group of Sanskrit letters, one can accomplish all the actions that one desires. One who is initiated should carry out the reverse Matrka and worship she who is Kula's support. Having known all, one becomes an expert having characteristics of the greatest strength.

PATALA 4

*I*n order to enter into the cosmic world of Matrka, the power of letters, it is necessary to be both well versed in Sanskrit and deeply absorbed in all the practices of the Kaula Way, which amounts to saying that the practice of Matrka is beyond reach. This practice alone would require twenty years of study, but fortunately, it can be adapted so that it is within the reach of serious practitioners. It is called the garland of letters. It is very useful for detoxing oneself from convictions, dogmas, and beliefs. This is the practice I'm going to transmit to you, but I will use Western letters. Matsyendranath says that the Kula pinda begins with *A* and finishes with *AH:* the first and last letters of the Sanskrit alphabet. So, you're going to begin with *A* and end with *Z*.

You are floating naked, seated in night-blue space.

You concentrate on the center between the eyebrows and you imagine that the letter *A*, colored red, emerges from your head, leaving through the center between the eyebrows. You see the letter *A* swooping around in space. Next you allow the letter *B* to spring forth, a beautiful yellow, and you see it dancing with the letter *A*. Following that you allow all the letters of the alphabet to emerge, each one of a beautiful color, and you let them move around in night-blue space in an unstructured way. This is the crazy dance of the *bijas,* the syllables, which you see clearly. They are like the bony structure of the language. You have before you all the possibilities of language without any meaning at all appearing out of them. This is the peaceful state of mind without form that we can call silence. At this stage, there is no inner dialogue; however, the entire potential of language is before your eyes, swooping around in the great silence.

You are now going to break the silence by saying a few words aloud that sum up one of your beliefs, such as, for example, "I believe in Shiva/Shakti."

The vowels *A, E, I, O, U* position themselves on a line and the other letters graft themselves onto this structure, forming the phrase "I believe in Shiva Shakti."

The other letters continue to fly around this central statement.

Repeat this statement slowly, trying to be aware of each letter as you're reading.

Enter the silence. The letters begin to move and change places, making a new sentence: "Ethli savik iba hivisene." Your certainty will begin to come apart when you try to read this sentence.

Now, imagine that the letters start to play with your thinking and arrange themselves in an order that sums up your belief, such as, for example, "sacralizations."

Set the letters flying again. All meaning is lost. You regain mental silence. Nothing remains but colors in space!

PRACTICE 9

Asceticism and Pleasuring

He who visualizes the beast (pashu, animal nature), which dissolves in the supreme lingam, which is the abode of flame, becomes independent and totally liberated. Everything that exists resides in his heart, since he knows all the qualities and is perfect like Bhairava.

PATALA 4

This practice allows you to bring together *bogha* (pleasuring) and yoga (asceticism). Reject nothing, but understand that the senses wander joyfully in their respective domains without experiencing the notion of purity or impurity. When the activity is *sahaja,* it implies mental silence and grace. You can allow your body total freedom in harmony with the cosmos. It will set in motion an activity of pleasuring united with the totality of each cell in the vibration of spanda. The *pashu,* that which manifests an unconscious energy of the totality by immersing itself in the supreme lingam becomes a *vira,* a hero. Thus, the flame of love rises up in night-blue space!

Lunar Nectar

We must meditate inwardly on a pure outburst of white light. This outburst must be refreshing, celestial, have a mellow scent, and it must extend off to infinity. It is the divine raison d'être of all refreshing libations of a lunar nature as well as being the center of space. It flows in us through all the many channels. By attaining that, we can have a long life and overcome death. The application of this method protects us from fever and from death; no one is ever again subject to disease or various ailments. Through this divine game, O Sweet-faced Lady, is bestowed the recompense of the siddhis. We must meditate, visualizing that in the middle of an Ocean of milk there is a great, pure lotus that is white. At the center of this lotus of 100,000,000,000 petals, the wise man visualizes his own being, while wearing white clothing and white ornaments. My Very Dear One, by meditating on the fact that we become one with this lotus, we have no need to feed ourselves! We must meditate on the rays that are white like milk while imagining that they are impregnating our minds. The rays liberate us from illness, from fever, from death, and from attachments. We can then play and enjoy ourselves in various ways, following our own will.

At present, I am going to reveal the whole doctrine specific to the victory over death. After having meditated on the dwelling place or seat of the Moon, and after having made contact with the higher Moon by meditating on the mind impregnated with the divine freshness of the lunar rays, we are liberated from fever, from death, and from all diseases. Through the application of this method over the course of one year, we will be assisted by the Kula yoginis.

Listen, O Kulabhavini Devi, to this other marvel! Meditate mentally on the Moon as being a Full Moon, entire and complete. You will never again know fever or illness. Kalyani Bhavini, now listen once again! We will meditate on the idea that this Moon resides in the navel, in the head, and in the heart. In practicing continually this way, so that we maintain ourselves constantly in a harmonious state of awareness during one year, we are completely liberated and separated from fever as well as from death. Once again, please listen carefully to this other method, O Lady Worshipped by the Viras! Meditate on the beautiful thousand-petalled lotus, which will be as white as pure cow's milk, just as if Devi was appearing in each of the chakras. In each of the chakras there flows an equal amount of lunar nectar and they are all sprinkled by the highest chakra. The yogi must continuously practice this sprinkling of his being with the nectar. He will then be liberated, avoiding old age and the slightest illness. He will be able to frolic in the ocean of samsara, My Very Dear One, for he will be fulfilled and will attain his independence.

There is another marvel, O Devi! Listen attentively. After having meditated on a sixteen-petalled lotus, snowy white like the color of the Moon, each petal being a sphere for Shiva's love games, we must visualize our own bodies bathed by the tide of nectar that flows over them, each one of these currents looking snowy white like the color of milk bathing our bodies and oozing from the pores. Then we will be like Shiva, no longer having to submit to fever, having no need of food, not knowing illness or death, completely independent, moving by our own will alone, and being adored by 100,000,000,000 gods and by numerous heavenly maidens. Devi, there are altogether eleven chakras plus the thousand-petalled chakra. They are located in the genitals, the navel, the heart, the throat, in the mouth, on the forehead, at the top of the cranium, in the bony joints of the cranium, and inside the Tridanda. Each one has 5, 8, 10, 12, 16, 100, and 10,000,000 petals, respectively.

Meditating on each one of the areas of the body confers various results. The color red always confers being all-powerful over others and a great serenity. Natha and yellow cause paralysis. Violet makes us always move far away. It is said that white ensures good health and has us also enjoy deep peace. It is said that the dazzling milky white color confers victory over death. With molten gold of dazzling brightness, we can make cities totter.

After having meditated on each of the chakras separately, considering that they are of a consistency similar to the original point, the cosmic sound, and Shakti, we obtain the grace of dharma, of artha, of kama, and of moksha, as well as anima and the eight other siddhis. Then we can see the future and have the power to create. There is no doubt that we can become like that through the constant practice of what has already been revealed. He who is initiated in the Kula Kaula Agama and who recites "the conqueror of death," O Devi, becomes, without any doubt, immortal and the guru of pious yoginis.

PATALA 5

*T*he moon bestows healing. The yoginis take moonlight baths to tonify their organs and stimulate the flow of that light in the subtle channels and chakras. It is an effective way of preventing illness and healing oneself when needed. The moon is powerful and beneficial. It balances all the subtle functions. The practices evoked here are equivalent and proceed with graduated intensity according to whether you take them in a more abstract way with the pure lunar milk or in a crazier way with the orgasmic pleasuring that emanates from the body of Shiva/Shakti. The sexual fluids have a great healing power. They are identical to lunar milk but arouse a more intense, passionate vibration. Practice by following your felt sense. Also practice according to the seasons or re-create the seasons in your body as a function of the moment. In winter, in an icy atmosphere for example, the intensity of the erotic passion of Shiva/Shakti will bring you the necessary fire. Conversely, during heat waves, the pure lunar milk will give you the impression that your nadis are run through with a thousand little rivers of incomparably cool freshness. Whichever your choice might be, the process is the same.

I'm going to speak to you now about the chakras. As pointed out in the *Spandakarika,** we always experience our beliefs, being careful not to use our experiences to validate our beliefs. In our yoga we ask the question: What would happen if we had no concept, no belief, no certainty? A fresh, unconditioned experience!

You are floating naked, seated in night-blue space.

Instead of imagining your chakras, be aware of the central channel that is like the stem of the lotus opening at the fontanel; it traverses the heart center and opens at the perineum. It is a tube of light connected to the cosmos. The breath will make the wheels

---

*See Daniel Odier, *Yoga Spandakarika: The Sacred Texts at the Origins of Tantra,* trans. Clare Frock (Rochester, Vt.: Inner Traditions, 2005).

appear, shaped as lotuses. Their number is not important. It is a natural burgeoning!

On the fontanel, the great lotus appears and on each petal Shiva/Shakti entwine and give themselves to love games with great sweetness, a great intensity in the slowness of their movements. The celestial nectar of their orgasmic pleasuring mixes and spreads through their bodies, bathing the nadis and flowing through all the pores of the skin, the yoni, and the lingam. This outpouring flows through you, in the central channel and in the lotuses that have appeared, as your whole body is soaked with the flow of orgasmic pleasuring of Shiva/Shakti. The nectar of love even courses through your bones. Your body is spatialized. Now, come back very gently and raise your eyelids like a curtain, very gradually.

The Three Moons

*Meditate mentally on the Moon as being a Full Moon, entire
and complete. You will never again know fever or illness.
Kalyani Bhavini, now listen once again! We will meditate
on the idea that this Moon resides in the navel, in the head,
and in the heart. In practicing continually this way, so that
we maintain ourselves constantly in a harmonious state of
awareness.*

PATALA 5

*Y*ou are floating in night-blue space. Facing you, a full moon
appears. It liquefies and enters you through the center
between the eyebrows. It enters into fullness again by taking
over the whole head. You concentrate on this full moon and it
gives birth to a second moon, which flows into your heart. This
moon grows and occupies the whole upper part of your torso.
It touches the base of the neck, the shoulder blades, and the
diaphragm.

A third moon breaks off and settles into your navel. It enlarges
until it reaches the perineum and includes the sexual organs.

The three moons are incandescent, they irradiate the bones,
muscles, nerves, tendons, organs, and, vivifying the nadis, the subtle channels.

The three moons barely touch each other. With each in-breath, they push your skin into space. With each out-breath, they come back toward the center.

This practice is very simple and should be done often, sometimes in a few minutes, anywhere and under any circumstances, because the body is sensitive to brief and repeated stimulation. There is no place that isn't conducive to this practice. Experiencing it is a great strength!

PRACTICE 12

The Flux of Lunar Nectar in the Chakras

Meditate on the beautiful thousand-petalled lotus, which will be as white as pure cow's milk, just as if Devi was appearing in each of the chakras. In each of the chakras, there flows an equal amount of lunar nectar and they are all sprinkled by the highest chakra. The yogi must continuously practice this sprinkling of his being with the nectar.

PATALA 5

*I*n this practice, as usual floating in night-blue space, imagine that each chakra, from head to toe, spins like a luminous spiral, distributing adamantine milk in each of your cells, in each muscle, each organ, each bone.

This is a very simple and very vivifying practice that you can do anywhere, even if just for a few seconds.

The energy descends in the form of a liquid spiral that moves through each chakra and departs from your body, taking all tensions with it.

This practice activates awareness of the central channel, which is Shakti. As is said in the *Vijnanabhairava Tantra:* "The central channel is the Goddess, like a lotus stem, red on the inside, blue on the outside. It moves through your body. By meditating on its inner void, you will reach a spatiality that is divine."*

---

*Odier, trans., *Tantra Yoga,* 17.

PRACTICE 13

The Flood Divine

*After having meditated on a sixteen-petalled lotus, snowy
white like the color of the Moon, each petal being a sphere for
Shiva's love games, we must visualize our own bodies bathed
by the tide of nectar that flows over them, each one of these
currents looking snowy white like the color of milk bathing our
bodies and oozing from the pores.*

PATALA 5

In night-blue space a sixteen-petalled lotus appears in your heart.
Shiva and Shakti manifest and multiply so that they are present on each petal. They entwine with each other as they exchange passionate kisses. Their bodies dance in loving ecstasy, skin lightly grazing skin, playfully penetrating each other through looks, through lips, chest, belly, and through sexual organs. Lingam penetrates yoni gently and slowly. They unite first of all in a lively way, then, once the fire is lit, they settle progressively into a movement that is barely visible. Orgasmic pleasuring flows continuously from yoni and lingam, and this flood divine begins to soak your whole body, each of your cells seeming to drink the orgasmic pleasuring of Shiva and Shakti. When your body is bathed all over with this liquid light, the orgasmic pleasuring begins to ooze through all the pores of your skin and spread into space around you. The cosmos becomes a flood of love that forms stars, planets, and vibrating masses, off into infinity.

PRACTICE 14

The Chakras

Devi, there are altogether eleven chakras plus the thousand-petalled chakra. They are located in the genitals, the navel, the heart, the throat, in the mouth, on the forehead, at the top of the cranium, in the bony joints of the cranium, and inside the Tridanda. Each one has 5, 8, 10, 12, 16, 100, and 10,000,000 petals, respectively.

Meditating on each one of the areas of the body confers various results. The color red always confers being all-powerful over others and a great serenity. Natha and yellow cause paralysis. Violet makes us always move far away. It is said that white ensures good health and has us also enjoy deep peace. It is said that the dazzling milky white color confers victory over death. With molten gold of dazzling brightness, we can make cities totter.

PATALA 5

𝒯he best practice for opening to the sensation of the wheels or chakras is to begin by coming aware of the central channel without arbitrarily locating the chakras in exact spots. The sensation must come from an open space in which the energy can manifest and begin to turn. That's why I'm speaking about wheels. You can visualize them like the waterwheels of a mill or like pinwheels, the colorful children's toys that are spun by the wind.

You are seated naked in night-blue space. From the fontanel to the perineum, you feel the central channel that is appearing. It is sometimes adamantine, sometimes red and blue as indicated in the *Vijnanabhairava Tantra*. Always let things happen. Everything that results from effort and concepts is an illusory and misleading sensation. Of course you can sense what you imagine, but I'm asking you to not imagine and instead to open the senses. What happens if the concept neither precedes nor follows the sensation? This is what our yoga is all about!

If the wheels appear, the number of petals of the different lotuses can vary. The numbers 5, 8, 10, 12, 16, 100, and 10,000,000 are only indications of possibilities. Listen in silence and let things happen very freely.

The lotuses flourish in the central channel. They take up their positions. They open.

Now, concentrate on the lotuses that are present. There may be 3, 8, 12—it doesn't matter.

Slip into your breathing and if the breathing moves through the central channel, what happens? The petals of the lotuses are going to curve inward as the breath rises and descends. There is going to be a successive movement of the petals of each lotus while at the same time adamantine light spreads through your body.

There remains only this very bright luminosity. The organs, muscles, nerves, tendons, and bones melt into the light.

The lotuses begin now to expand. They extend horizontally in your body, moving beyond it and forming a sphere in which the lotuses are floating horizontally. The breath extends them to infinity and you see your body at the center of the cosmos with each successive wheel. You become the center of these immense chakras, which are floating like jellyfish.

Remain in this state of openness.

Now imagine that the lotuses are returning, little by little, toward the central channel, carrying back with them the memory of infinite space.

Little by little, the organs, the muscles, and the bones reappear.

You return to your body once again through the sensation of space.

This practice should be done often, regardless of where you are. Vary the duration of the practice frequently: one minute, seven minutes, a half hour. In peaceful spots, in bustling spots. Alone or with others.

PRACTICE 15

Lineage Yoga

*According to the uninterrupted succession of masters, through
oral transmission, O Devi, it resides in the navel, the heart,
the mouth, and the nostrils. This is Kaulika knowledge, O
Devi, which has been transmitted to us by the oral tradition.*

PATALA 6

*H*ere we come to a crucial point: There cannot be either transmission or practice without being connected to the lineage
of masters. The practice is so essential that it is considered to be
already known and integrated by the practitioner. The *Kaulajnana*
is the ultimate tantra, the royal way, the highest of the practices
that have remained secret for a long time. They allow the last
veils and the connection to ego to be torn away through a striking
descent of grace coming from the masters. There are a number of
ways of practicing lineage yoga depending on the level of the disciple, the circumstances, the moment. I am providing for you here
one of the most beautiful and most profound:

You are floating, naked, seated in night-blue space. Your
breathing becomes established and begins to make your bodily
shape fluctuate; it dilates into space and comes back toward
the heart.

You call forth my presence by a fervent leap forward
toward space.

I come and position myself on your fontanel. I am the size of your head and my body is very luminous. You can see this in detail—my face, my body, my light, or you may simply feel my presence.

Above me, on my head, my master Sahajanandabhairava is positioned. Then, the yoginis and mahasiddhas of the Kaula tradition. They are pure presences and you will see that, with practice, two or three of these yoginis and these masters will become more and more familiar. You will recognize them by how they look at you and by their faces, their clothing, their perfumes. The yoginis and the masters always exude an enchanting perfume. This is the simplest and most animal way of recognizing a master. These two or three members of the lineage will be your guardians, your protectors, and—as it has been for me—they will continue to teach through dreams at night and waking dreams within the interstitial emptiness that breaks up reality. These vikalpas (dreams, illusions) are spoken about in the *Vijnanabhairava Tantra*. Death never separates masters and disciples. It's simply another means of communication that gets established. You are never alone. You are part of this infinite chain that transmits knowledge and the carrying out of the teachings.

The whole lineage melts and flows into your heart through the fontanel and the central channel. This energy compacts down into a gold sphere of small dimensions that resides in your heart. Focus on this sphere.

With your breath, you project this sphere into night-blue space opposite you a few yards away.

The sphere enlarges and there appears within it Shiva/Shakti in their androgynous, golden form. You study them, fascinated. One breast, two sets of sexual organs, and a harmonious face where feminine and masculine blend.

The yoginis and the mahasiddhas spring forth from their single heart like clouds of butterflies, arranging themselves all around them in night-blue space. A phenomenal energy emerges from all these bodies.

The whole lineage returns into the body of Shiva/Shakti, shining with extreme brilliance.

The androgynous body embraces you, holding you tightly, heart to heart, lips to lips, eyes to eyes. The sexual organs touch.

Shiva/Shakti give you breathing, your lips take it in from their lips. It descends into your heart, into your sexual organs, returning back into the body of Shiva/Shakti in an energy that revolves more and more quickly becoming more and more luminous. Little by little, your body is continually traversed by this spherical current in which breathing and sexual energy mix. This ring of light, little by little, absorbs the bodies. There remains only this revolving in the center of night-blue space.

The energy compacts into a sphere that explodes, giving birth to stars and galaxies.

Amrita, the Divine Nectar

O Lady! What you are asking of me remains very mysterious. Without any doubt, I am speaking about what liberates us from death. We must satiate ourselves with amrita, the divine nectar, the very essence of Brahma. After a month, one can vanquish death. It is true! By placing amrita at the root of the palate, one must gradually ingest the breath of life. O Devi! After six months of diligent practice, liberation from the direst illnesses will spring forth. Practicing for a year makes us healthy and frees us from death. One can even see into the future and be able to hear words spoken far away. Venom cannot stay in the body even if one has a serious illness. When the mind is settled, one is liberated from all poisons, whether fixed or moving, even if the skin is cut open. Between the two is found Rajada, the central place, the bindu itself.

Amrita regenerates us. It produces youth and destroys old age. The wise man, having produced a drink of fresh amrita in this place, is freed from wrinkles and white hair. He is freed of all illness.

Patala 6

A mrita is the essential nutrient of the yoginis. It is produced when the state of samadhi stabilizes. Amrita is not the first saliva, but what comes afterward. Its consistency is different—

more oily, more scented, more abundant. This elixir can also come into the sexual juices when you are in a state of union with all that is. The second saliva is delicious and is an indication of a state of inner happiness. If you concentrate on the oral cavity and relax the tongue, you will see that it spontaneously comes to flow over the palate before stopping behind the upper teeth. But do not think about it—just relax and see what your tongue is going to do. If you place your tongue right on the palate, the tongue tenses. Everything happens by itself in our yoga. Awareness instead of will. You can lick in order to heal, as many yoginis do. You can use your orgasmic pleasuring to heal. These are secret things that few practitioners know about and which can only take place in an ecstatic state. All our practices have samadhi as their foundation. Without it, you have nothing but gestures, movements, and concepts that are empty of meaning. When the amrita flows in torrents, you are nourished, you can consume food much more sparingly, survive in the cold or in a hostile natural environment—deserts, frozen lands—like an animal reconnecting with its instinct, with its connection to nature. Don't ever try to stop eating—that's not an end in itself. Don't try to fly or disappear. There are siddhis that are much simpler to attain. In your presence, you can be a plant, an animal, a mineral, the sky, the wind, ether. These are easy siddhis. The most important siddhi is your ability to blend into reality with grace, spontaneity, and lightness. That is the state of sahaja!

The Color Black

Sweet-faced One! We are going to visualize the top of the head in a white color, like the Moon, as if a lake of the purest ghee is nourishing the chakra of the bones. One must meditate on the top of the cranium where there's a black mark from which an ointment is flowing, destroying wrinkles and gray hair. From now on, O Devi! Listen carefully to the second method. At the spot where, from the point of view of yoga, there is located the stem of the Adhara chakras, which is cool, fresh, and dissolves in the Brahmarandhra, one must visualize the flow of the black ointment. One must know that, by nature, the Sun is hostile and the Moon is friendly. By meditating on a single black spot as well as by wearing black clothing, one can be freed of all the setbacks and confusions generated by life, and freed of all the ills.

P ATALA 7

*Y*ou are floating naked in night-blue space and after making the moon flow in you, you move on with no transition to having the black ointment flow in you.

Black in our tradition is loved by the yoginis, who don't see it as an absence of color but, on the contrary, the bringing together of all colors, as in a handful of volcanic sand where the sparkling yellows, blues, violets, and reds are like nuggets that glitter so much more by being surrounded by darkness.

Black or night-blue is also the body of Kali, who comes dancing in us in all her splendor. It is her infinite love that flows in you and when you see me as Kali, it is I who glides in your body's light, bringing peace and love.

You are like Kamadeva, the god of love, by uniting with the place where yoginis dwell, while you meditate on them and on yourself as being black in color.

When you are practicing with the red goddesses, there arrives a moment when the black goddesses, who are even more impressive, come bringing a coloration that will undo fears linked to outer darkness and to your own inner darkness. The black goddesses will annihilate the fear of descending into dark areas, into instincts and ancient powers at humanity's roots, the zone that defies all description, but which harbors fabulous energy. Black is not the absence of color and form; it is the reservoir of our fundamental humanity and of a lifesaving wildness that we have forgotten about. The Kali Yuga is characterized also by this fear of entering into the heart of the world in order to find nuggets of beauty there. Enter Kali! *Rim shrim Krim Parameshvari Kalike svaha!*

PRACTICE 18

The Lunar River

Let us meditate on the image of an eight-petalled chakra, colored white like the Moon, and located where the spine meets the skull, that is, where one's hairline begins. We can gratify our bodies thanks to this light.

PATALA 7

*Y*ou are floating naked, seated in night-blue space. Your breathing is becoming more and more finely subtle. It transforms into a breathing cycle that forms an energy loop moving across your palate, descending along the central channel, looping around the perineum, and coming back up in front of the spine. Behind you a magnificent full moon appears. You feel its rays shining on your skin, but you cannot see it. Your desire to rest your gaze upon it is so great that you imagine that your eyes turn back slowly and focus on the spot of the secret chakra found in the occiput, where your hairline begins. With your finger, you can feel a slight hollow there. A triangle is formed, joining your left eye, your right eye, and the secret chakra that will gradually open so you can see the moon. You gaze at it until the moment when a river of lunar milk emerges from the moon, enters your secret chakra, sprinkling the eight-petalled lotus and spreading out impetuously through your head, irrigating your brain with a milky whiteness and carrying away all the dark shadows of suffering, memories, and patterns of conditioning. The tumultuous flow descends through your body, moving through the bones, muscles, organs, nerves, and tendons, carrying with it all traces of darkness. The river of milky light revolves in your pelvic area, touching all parts and moving out into night-blue space continuously until you become nothing but lunar light. Stay in this space until the lunar river ceases to enter you. The secret chakra that opened now closes. Your eyes return to where they belong. The river leaves your body. Be aware of your luminous spatiality and gently come back to where you are, slowly opening your eyes.

PRACTICE 19

The Sahaja Mothers, the Heart Practice of the Yoginis

The Sahaja Mothers of Devi are very powerful and very terrifying. They are beautiful and red in color. They allow even a pashu to attain a celestial state. These Mothers give birth to living beings. They are behind the genesis of the being in the womb.

*They are called Brahmi, Maheshvari, Kaumari, Vaisnavi, Varahi, Vajrahasta, Yogeshvari, and Aghoresi. It has to do with the famous Matrka, which emanates from Devi, it is said.**

PATALA 8

*T*his is the practice that was transmitted from Shambunatha to Abhinavagupta, allowing him to attain enlightenment. This practice leads to the ultimate, which is why it is barely mentioned here. It is also called the heart practice of the yoginis.

Imagine that you are floating, seated and naked, in night-blue space. Let your breathing emerge through an attention concentrated on the in-breath by thoroughly relaxing the deep

---

*On the eight goddesses and Durga, see the fascinating book by Laura Amazzone, *Goddess Durgā and Sacred Female Power* (Lanham, Md.: Hamilton, 2010), 117–18.

muscles of the lower belly and slacken your attention on the out-breath, which will happen all on its own. Constant attention to the breathing tires one unhelpfully. You can also choose to do the opposite. Concentration on the full out-breath without any effort when the in-breath happens. This is something we do in most of the practices so as to remain in a state of relaxation, without forcing, without trying, just a natural process in which awareness replaces effort. This is the fundamental contribution of the yoginis.

As numerous tantras imply, the heart is the principal energy center in the Kaula Way. The Heart Practice of the yoginis is considered the ultimate practice of the sadhaka because it cease-lessly connects him to the energy of the heart by creating with the world perceived in its reality a whirlwind that ceaselessly feeds the energy of the heart. Reality and absolute therefore fuse. This is the secret practice of the sixty-four yoginis who make the eight chakras vibrate. This is the summit of the way leading to the incomparable, the discovery of the limitless. "The heart is the Goddess," says Abhinavagupta.

The energy of the heart whirls ceaselessly. Red goddesses emerge from it, harvesting the Real and bringing back intimate substance into the practitioner's heart. The heart is like a hive and the red goddesses are like bees extracting pollen from flowers and bringing it back to nourish the queen of the heart. This continu-ous springing forth gives rise to eternal happiness and spanda. It dissolves the ego's knots and brings deliverance. The heart is also called Shakti chakra. So there is a double spiral that emerges from and returns to the heart center.

This practice leads to constant integration of the Real into the heart center.

Abhinavagupta points out that pleasures of the senses linked to ego empty the heart's reservoir, while the practice of the red goddesses constantly refills it.

There are, however, three obstacles to move beyond:

- The obstacle of egoic individuality.
- The obstacle of not recognizing one's fullness and one's being divine.
- The obstacle that makes sensory pleasures a distraction, a loss of absolute essence instead of a return to the heart.

Attachment is an identification with the physical body; liberation is an identification with the cosmic body.

Abhinavagupta says that he who at every instant dissolves the universe in his own awareness and then manifests it again by projecting toward the world becomes Bhairava/Bhairavi.

- Be aware that reality is identical to your own heart, the place where the red yoginis reside.
- Levels of reality wrap around absolute consciousness.
- The fire of the knowing subject and the experience under the aspect of the sun and the moon of the known object form a spiral that is poured into the heart and emerges from it ceaselessly.
- Reality dissolves in the fire of the heart. It springs forth from it.
- The ceaseless whirling reveals the true nature of the Self.
- The Shakti chakra of the heart enjoys all sensory, emotional, and mental forms, and the goddesses ceaselessly harvest reality to dissolve it in the heart.
- Exterior objects are recognized as identical to absolute consciousness in the fire of nonduality.

- The traces and residues of the perceptions dissolve.
- This is the union of Bhairava/Bhairavi in the heart.
- Through this practice we attain supernatural powers that coincide perfectly with the Real.

When the identity of the cosmos and your own heart have been clearly perceived, you gently come back to where you are and you open your eyes abruptly.

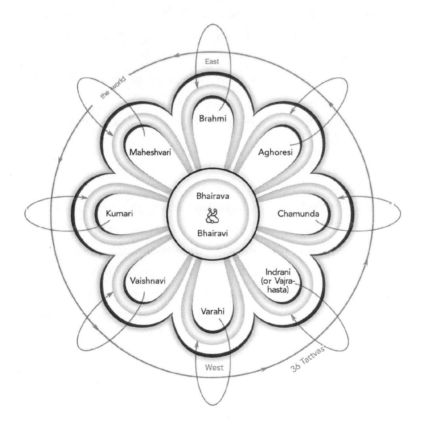

Brahmi, Maheshvari, Kumari, Vaishnavi, Varahi, Indrani (or Vajrahasta), Chamunda, Aghoresi

Illustration by Michael Marschner

PRACTICE 20

The Eight Chakras

The letter "Ksa" is located in the Brahmarandhra, "La" in the forehead, "Ha" between the eyes, "Sa" in the mouth, "Sha" in the throat, "Sha" in the heart, "Va" in the navel, and "Hla" in the genitals.

My Dear One! Learn the meditation on the placement of these chakras.

The first of the eight chakras is a celestial eight-petalled lotus, like a pure limpid crystal, a divine flame or fire, lacking any imperfection. It is free of all duality, free of the flames of cruelty, and even stripped of the void. We must avoid the slightest disruption and put sama consciousness into practice. From then on, we are able to make out the future, having united with the unshakable circle of time. We can know what is spoken great distances away, we can confer favors and paralyze others, we can seize and subjugate pashus, or destroy them or kill them, we can be immortal, always truthful and balanced, eloquent like the siddhas, and able to fulfill our desires.

We must meditate on the second eight-petalled chakra, which is also as brilliant as a beautiful pure flame. In this way, we can vanquish death and be at the start of great tumult. By meditating calmly on this complex form, one becomes an emperor among kings, one who can accomplish everything one wants. Always engaged in the path of love, being similar to Kruddha—such a one can destroy everything in the three worlds, living beings as well as inanimate objects.

The third chakra is the one that gives birth to nine tattvas. After having meditated for six months on the guru, who is situated in this adhara, we can accomplish whatever we desire: the effects of old age are destroyed, one is able to see far into the distance and immobilize others even from a distance of one hundred yojanas. In a solitary spot we must meditate on this complex form.

The fourth chakra is the source of peace. It increases happiness and contentment. In always meditating on it, we become immortal, eloquent, and victorious over death and illness. The daily practice of it sends death flying. An ongoing practice on this great chakra, during a period of sixteen seasons, makes it possible to generate destruction in one day and one night. O Surasundari!

The fifth great lotus has eight petals. We must always meditate on it as being the color of smoke, and then it becomes possible to shake the foundations of the Three Worlds. It generates eloquence and avoids untimely death. It allows one to both enslave and to paralyze.

If we meditate with devotion on the sixth royal chakra, which is all ablaze and has a pericarp of eight petals that is as luminous as molten gold and is (considered to be) the source of Iccha Siddhi, we can see the future, obtain the anima and seven other siddhis. About that there is no doubt, Dear Mahadevi!

The seventh chakra is as luminous as the Full Moon and is propitious. Inside the body, it confers both happiness and liberation. It destroys fever and death, and it allows you to penetrate the bodies of others. What cannot be accomplished? One becomes the best within a group of individuals.

Beautiful to contemplate! The eighth chakra is embellished with eight petals. It confers dharma, artha, kama, and moksha.

When we meditate on the chakras as being red, they always confer authority over others. If yellow, they cause paralysis. If pure crystal, they confer liberation and, if black, then death. If the color of smoke, they give the power to uproot. In meditating on them being a white that is as pure as cow's milk, one obtains Mrtyuinjaya. One can cause great tumult, paralysis; cause the intellectual and physical abilities of others to be lost; and many other things.

PATALA 10

Matsyendranath, faithful to the tantra tradition, gives information about the chakras that seems contradictory. He tells us eight when he's speaking of the sixty-four yoginis, or eleven, or further along twelve plus the secret chakra located at the occiput. Depending on each practice, one feels different manifestations. One can feel the whole central channel as a single chakra of light, blue on the outside and red inside. One may feel only the wheel of the heart. It's better to think of them as wheels because they rotate, and in all these practices the dynamic is very important. To make things simpler, concentrate on the eight chakras and then let other possible manifestations well up freely.

1. The fontanel chakra, the color of flaming crystal. It corresponds to the Sanskrit letter "*Ksa.*"

   "The first chakra confers the power to unite with the yoginis, the power to make oneself small, and among the eight siddhis effective attainment in meditation and sadhana."*

---

*All the notes on the chakras that are in quotes are from Matsyendranath in Patala 8.

2. The chakra in the middle of the forehead, the color of pure flame. It corresponds to the Sanskrit letter "*La*."

"With the puja and the dhyana (meditation) centered on the second chakra, one acquires the power to hypnotize all beings, the ability to break or throw objects at a distance, and the ability to subjugate others."

3. The between-the-eyebrows chakra, the color of diamond. It corresponds to the Sanskrit letter "*Ha*."

"Whoever practices frequently the method of the third great chakra can subtly slip into someone else's body and, in addition, he is able to access visions of the future."

4. The chakra of the palate and the mouth. Its color is pink. It corresponds to the Sanskrit letter "*Sa*."

"The fourth chakra is a marvelous provider of the powers of calming, liberation, and sensual pleasuring. If one venerates this chakra using a person's image during meditation, one is capable of instantly paralyzing someone with a single gesture. In addition, one gains the power of invisibility and of hearing conversations whether they are nearby or distant."

5. The chakra of the throat. It is the color of smoke. It corresponds to the Sanskrit letter "*Sha*."

"By meditating and carrying out sadhana on the fifth great chakra, one is capable of speaking like a rishi, moving like the wind, and halting someone's conversation."

6. The chakra of the heart. It is the color of liquid gold. It corresponds to the Sanskrit letter "*Sha*."

"The sixth chakra bestows dharma (teaching), artha (power), and moksha (liberation)."

7. The chakra of the navel. It is the color of the full moon. It corresponds to the Sanskrit letter "*Va*."

"Whoever practices and attains his sadhana on the seventh

chakra for long periods will obtain the power to enslave others . . . he will liberate himself from the chains of samsara."

8. The perineal or sexual chakra. It is the color of red gold. It corresponds to the Sanskrit letter "*Hla.*"

"The eighth chakra is the vehicle that sets Iccha Siddhi in motion. In addition, it allows one to cause death and to travel far away, and moreover it bestows the power to generate paralysis or illusion in others. He who is established in this great chakra is beloved by the Kulas, by the yoginis. It is only by being aware of the sixty-four rules that the siddhis are granted, otherwise they are not granted. The secret order of the sixty-four yoginis has thus been stated by me, and I have done so in the clearest of terms. You must remember this with devotion."

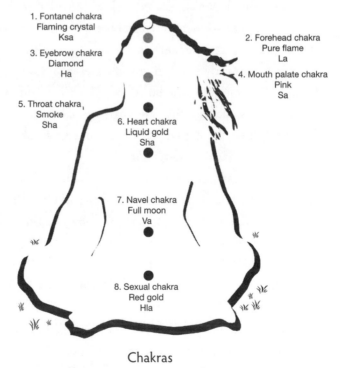

1. Fontanel chakra
Flaming crystal
Ksa

2. Forehead chakra
Pure flame
La

3. Eyebrow chakra
Diamond
Ha

4. Mouth palate chakra
Pink
Sa

5. Throat chakra
Smoke
Sha

6. Heart chakra
Liquid gold
Sha

7. Navel chakra
Full moon
Va

8. Sexual chakra
Red gold
Hla

Chakras

Illustration by Michael Marschner

PRACTICE 21

The Eight Red Goddesses and the Chakras

One should always meditate on the eight chakras with the help of a beautiful, intense, and luminous flame that one moves eight times, one by one, through each of the centers. Through one's own willpower, one becomes the Lord of Breath capable of generating enthusiasm by being united with Kanchuki Devi herself.

PATALA 10

*Y*ou are floating naked, seated in night-blue space. Visualize the eight chakras in the order and placement explained in the preceding practice. An intense flame coming from space settles on the center of the fontanel, on the petal that protrudes opposite you, that of Brahmi. The flame moves slowly on to the second petal, that of Maheshvari, then that of Kumari. It settles next on that of Vaishnavi, that of Varahi, that of Vajrahasta, that of Chamunda or Yogeshvari, and finally the eighth, that of Aghoresi.* It's your breath that makes the flame rotate. Little by little, the pace increases, always turning counterclockwise— we always turn to the left, in the direction of the heart. What's most important in this practice is that it pulls the whole cosmos

---

*On the Matrka and the eight goddesses, see Amazzone, *Goddess Durgā and Sacred Female Power,* 116–19.

into its dizzying gyration. The energy circulates like a spiral that descends progressively from one chakra to the next. Connect all the lotuses all the way down to the base chakra, and when you feel the spiral moving through you and you feel pulled into this spiral of fire, imagine that it begins far out in space above you and that it departs through the base chakra, losing itself in night-blue space. The whirlwind gradually accelerates. It connects each center to the others. Little by little, the energy makes you aware of the central channel, which has become a whirlwind of light. In winter, visualize the flames being a beautiful, intense red. In summer, instead see them white, like a refreshing diamond.

Another especially important practice is dedicated to the goddess Kaumari (Kumari). She is the one of the eight goddesses who is especially auspicious when we begin a practice in the morning. She presides over the ritual bath that we often conduct in the imagination rather than plunging ourselves into sacred waters. Once we have a deep understanding of the Kaula Way, everything is sacred. There is no longer any distinction between sacred and profane, pure and impure, chaotic or ordered. If you want a sacred bath, the yoni is the most beautiful of rivers, equal to the Ganges in its pouring out from an ejaculation of Shiva!

The goddess I am speaking about is Kaumari—a very beautiful adolescent, red, transparent. She is capricious, gentle, impetuous, without limits. She can sometimes be terrifying, but in this practice it is through her extreme gentleness that you will come to know her.

You are seated on a rock that is flat and round, protruding just above the surface of the water in the middle of a Himalayan lake. You can see the snowy peaks, the starry sky, and a crescent moon.

You have just sat down on this flat rock. You dip lightly into the cool and reinvigorating water.

You gaze at the shore.

A sparkling ruby appears, floating in space. It mesmerizes you. You concentrate all your attention on it until it suddenly transforms into the splendid and transparent body of Kaumari. If you see the beauty of her features, of her curves, of her red nakedness, and of her black hair that reaches down to her knees, that's marvelous. If you only perceive a red energy, that's fine too. Goddesses don't appear immediately. You have to deserve them—you have to open to them. They are modest and delicate, and don't show themselves to anyone who doesn't deeply adore them.

Kaumari begins the Tandava dance on the waters with grace and infinite slowness. She approaches little by little and her features become more and more distinct.

She comes and sits down opposite you. Her red, mellow energy penetrates into you. She smiles at you. Her whole body expresses benevolence.

Kaumari brings her hands together over her heart as if to greet you.

Little by little she lowers her hands.

The tips of her fingers settle delicately on your navel.

Very gently she enters into your body. The sensation is marvelous.

With her delicate hands she makes her way among the organs, encircling an organ in the lower body like the prostate or the uterus. It is very important in this practice to always perceive your body as being whole. Nothing has ever been removed. That will allow you to recover the sensation of missing organs and to make energy circulate in them.

Slowly, Kaumari will remove the organ from your body and plunge it into the cool water. As soon as it is immersed, the organ relaxes, releases its toxins, its memories, its trauma. It recovers its freshness and its innocence. It takes on light colors.

Kaumari comes back into your body. She removes another organ, a kidney for example, and plunges it into the cool water of the lake.

She continues in this way, moving upward while you gaze at the beauty of your organs around the circular stone. They are recovering vitality and color.

Kaumari removes the intestines, the lungs, the diaphragm, the liver, the spleen, the pancreas, the heart, the tongue, the eyes, and finally, the brain.

As soon as the brain is in the water, it is emptied of its memories and its conditioning. It is like the brain of a newborn.

You are mesmerized by the beauty of all your organs as they communicate with you marvelously.

Kaumari begins then to replace them in your body in the order with which she removed them.

As soon as three or four have been replaced, you feel a new communication, a quivering spreading through your body.

When Kaumari puts the brain back, everything reconnects and begins working marvelously. There are no longer any obstacles. You are sensitive to the perception that your body is a totality, and that it is divine.

In order to celebrate this state, Kaumari jumps on your thighs and presses against your body. Your two hearts are now one. Skin touches skin, the two bodies enter into each other.

You become Kaumari. There is now only one breath, only one red presence in the middle of the lake.

After tasting union, Kaumari, with a powerful out-breath, pushes you out of her body and you find yourself facing her on the stone.

She rises gracefully and begins once again the Tandava dance on the waters.

She moves away. You watch her go.

Suddenly, she becomes the ruby once again.

You gaze at the ruby until it disappears in night-blue space.

PRACTICE 22

Eternal Substances

In the Kaula Agama the five eternal and pure substances are ashes, woman's nectar, sperm, blood, and clarified butter all mixed together.

PATALA 11

*J*t is essential in sadhana to explore ancestral, cultural, religious, and social taboos and fears. Our way is always characterized by its acceptance of all human beings, regardless of their condition, rank, culture, or social status. The outcasts, the rejected ones, even enjoy a privileged position. Even a Brahmin must return to the rank of untouchable in order to be admitted into Kaula circles. Matsyendranath, Abhinavagupta, and many other masters were Brahmins who gave up their privileges in order to merge into the sphere where each human being radiates their own splendor.

Among the most powerful fears affecting nearly all men, whether they're religious or not, the fear of menstrual blood is one of the most powerful. Religious men banish the lunar woman to a no-contact area. In the culture of India, a woman cannot touch anything during this period. It is said that she pollutes everything. For the yoginis, it's exactly the opposite. During that time the woman incarnates the whole power of Shakti. She is at her energetic and spiritual peak and any man who has the chance to taste her red nectar would be immediately pushed into the goddess's sphere. The taboo of the woman's orgasm, so powerful at that time, is not as strong but it also seems to be disconcerting for men. The amrita may be white or red, two sacred colors. By tasting these two springs, the cells discover spanda. For women, there is also the taboo or the fear of sperm, the taste of which, however, indicates the level of practice of the tantrika. Repeated samadhi renders it mellow and delicious with a perfume of the Mohana flower and a taste of mango.

Ashes are what remains of the black and they are brightening up. Ghee is clarified butter. Sometimes I mix these five sacred ingredients in order to adorn your forehead with *tika!*

PRACTICE 23

Dietary Prescriptions

My Dear One! From now on, one can eat whatever one wants.
One should have wine and eat as much as one wants in order
to have a long life. Three kinds of cakes should be offered, as
well as various kinds of fruit and lemons. According to the
rule, it is necessary to offer wine made from the fruit of trees,
roots, or flowers as an oblation to the devatas. In the course
of rites for specific desires, it is necessary to offer meat, wine,
and sweetened alcohol. One must observe nonduality here and
never do otherwise.

Patala 11

*J*n the Kaula Way there are these dietary prescriptions founded
on the idea of nonduality, the non-separation of things. In
order to become one with the totality, you have to devour the
totality. In contrast to the Hindu view, there is nothing in the
Kaula Way that is either pure or impure. We are not limited by
any theory. We are nourished according to the circumstances, the
location, the season, and the offerings we receive. For us, everything is awareness and vibration. Everything is alive. Everything
is the consequence of a vast system of reciprocal consuming. The
earth, which produces vegetables and grains, is nourished by thousands of minuscule animals that live and die in order to give birth
to a sprout of rice or a carrot, and these foods are nourished by

dead animals. There is a perpetual cycle in which each thing exists thanks to the whole, the totality. This, then, gives rise to the idea that we must nourish ourselves from the totality. Consider this rather clear statement: *Anyone who is satisfied offering only vegetarian food incurs three additional incarnations.* When you breathe the scent of a flower, you breathe the infinite cycle of life and death. You cannot escape this. The Kaula Way is first and foremost the way of absolute freedom and spontaneity—the way of the nonmental body. Therefore, disconnected from any judgment or mental activity, simply ask your body what it wants. The body knows. "A simple nondual approach is needed," says Matsyendranath. At the end of the patala on diet, there are these lines:

> *One is praised by the siddhas for seeing and touching Shakti's blood, as well as for the sexual pleasure from knowing the Kula Way for six months. My Very Dear One! A Brahmin goes to heaven thanks to endless ablutions of his feet and mouth, whereas he who often makes a tilaka of kunda, a gola or an udbhava of blood can destroy various illnesses such as leprosy and smallpox. He is freed of all sickness in the same way a serpent sheds his skin when molting. Such a being is as brilliant as the sun at its zenith and is beloved by the yoginis. He is equal to the Absolute, the Conqueror of Three Worlds, who performs oblation only by following the way of nonduality. Devi, one must accomplish all that resides in Iccha Shakti and not offer oblation unless it be in accord with Will. Oblation according to the nondual way has thus been declared in the* Jnana Nirnaya Tantra.

This means that the sexual fluids and menstrual blood of Shakti have a strong healing power, and that the vira who dares to worship their substance can escape all kinds of illnesses through an alchemical process. But for this, one must be a worshipper of the feminine in oneself! As is said in the *Kularnava Tantra:* "*Values are turned upside down in the Kula Way. What is rejected in the ordinary world is worshipped here and what is worshipped in the ordinary world is rejected here.*"*

---

*Translation by Arthur Avalon, Motital Banarsidass, 2007.

PRACTICE 24

Freedom

O Resplendent One! The way is to act according to one's own will, while being aware of both the Akula and Devi's Kula.

PATALA 12

*T*he highest attainment of the Kaula Way is to reach the state of sahaja, innate and spontaneous freedom that is engaged beyond thought, beyond social boundaries, and beyond cultural conditioning. This freedom is founded on identifying with the divine, with the cosmos. The state of sahaja is a state of grace, of joy, of union with all that is, freed from forms, rituals, beliefs, and dogmas. It is a residing in inner silence strongly anchored in a body-space, a sensitive, living, quivering body that obeys the world directly.

PRACTICE 25

Hamsa

In the animate and inanimate worlds, one should always recite "Hamsa Hamsa." Having heard this, one becomes fortunate like a Lord of Heaven who has gained the opportunity of spiritual liberation. The Three Worlds and the Cosmos emanate from this great wonder, which remains stable in eternity. After becoming aware of this great secret, one knows everything. By this means only, beings are liberated. All actions would be futile without it. In being distanced from that, one will never know what is auspicious or inauspicious. Without this, neither mind nor citta exist. Taste or meditation will not be able to exist. Those who know this are freed from mind and non-mind. When we perceive the phenomenon, that is, the letters of Hamsa, in the thousand-petalled lotus, it appears like a garland of joyous blossoms. Anyone who becomes like this is freed from merit and demerit. He progresses on the grand path of divinity and enjoys full awareness. There is no doubt about this.

PATALA 13

$\mathcal{T}$he "Hamsa" mantra is inner, like all forms of Kaula. "Ha" is Shiva, "Sa" is Shakti. Hamsa celebrates their union in the body. Hamsa is at one and the same time the creative act and all objects of creation. It is the perpetual breath, the ascendent and descendent rhythm, and the vibration that results from that. It is transmitted from mouth to mouth, murmured on your lips so it flows directly to your heart. It is the expression of the unity of all things. It is ajapa, that is: silent. It is simply a movement of awareness incarnated by the breath.

PRACTICE 26

Samadhi of the Heart and the Rainbow Body

After having meditated on the center of one's heart, one is then settled there. From then on, one can obtain samadhi, paralyze and subjugate others, and so forth. All that, while experiencing a sensation of vibration in the hands, the head, the feet—in fact, in the whole body.

PATALA 14

*T*he Bhairavi energy is in me. It is that energy that is going to introduce you to the spheres and to the rainbow body. At a certain depth of practice, visions of the natural state of mind will manifest in you. Springing up from the depth of the silent mind that returns to the mother, to the uterus of Bhairavi from the heart/mind, the visions will manifest during non-meditation. They will resemble the practice of the *Vijnanabhairava Tantra* that you love so much, the one in which you gaze at the colored circles of the peacock's feather. *"Imagine the five colored circles of a peacock feather as being the five senses spread through limitless space and residing in the spatiality of your own heart."**

The heart is the seat of the natural state. Visions and rainbows spring forth and manifest your body in a dimension of spa-

---

*Odier, trans., *Tantra Yoga,*17.

66

tiality. The natural state is the union of appearances and space. The heart is the source of all things; coming back to it is mystical accomplishment. There is nothing to be found outside of it. Even in moments of turmoil, always come back to your source. The heart is also the chamber of love in which we always find ourselves again, beyond limits of space and time. Your heart is my heart. You find yourself in me and I find myself in you. No thing and no one will be able to disturb this sacred union. Bhairava and Bhairavi! The visions are the prelude to the practice of the rainbow body that is to be done at the moment of dying.

"You are floating, seated, naked, in night-blue space.

Your breathing is very slow, deep, almost imperceptible. You are breathing through your mouth.

You gaze far away and it takes you into night-blue space.

Your gaze becomes space.

A diamond appears in the distance, the size of a fingertip. It sparkles.

Your fascination with the diamond draws it toward your heart. It moves through space.

The diamond settles on your skin in the middle of your chest.

With your breathing you draw it into your own heart, in the center of your upper body.

Little by little, the diamond lights up your organs, your muscles, your tendons, and your bones.

Light takes up resonance in you. You are now nothing but luminous space.

Your skin becomes transparent. It spreads out with the breathing, then comes back toward the heart.

In the heart of the diamond, a rainbow appears. Colors spring forth from its center and rotate counterclockwise because the heart is to the left. We always circumambulate sacred sites this way, but no site is as sacred as your own body because your body is All That Is.

Little by little, the whirlwind in the heart begins to well up from the diamond and multiple rainbows begin to travel throughout your body very freely until they fill it completely. You become only rainbows at the center of night-blue space.

With great gentleness, the rainbows push your skin toward infinity.

You allow this expansion to happen naturally. It can take you very far away or remain a few yards away. Sometimes it will lead you into absolute union with space.

Since your body is mine, experience infinite space now.

PHAT!

Space-Time dilates to the extreme in the rainbow samadhi.

Now the diamond absorbs the rainbows that are whirling through it before disappearing. The rainbows carry the memory of infinite space into your body, your organs, your muscles, your tendons, your bones, and into all the bodily fluids. Everything reappears gently. The colors are light and transparent, vibrant and sweet."

PRACTICE 27

The Throat and the God of Love

After having established one's consciousness in the well of the throat center, one can proclaim and describe the true essence of the shastras, thanks to one's own Shakti. One may see beyond the future, as well as the infinite circle of time and space, becoming free from death, strong, immortal, and radiant, liberated from fever and other illnesses, liberated from physical degeneration. Like Kruddha, one gains the ability to shake the Three Worlds and all that is found there, animate beings or inanimate objects. He who puts this method into practice will not only be the equal of Brahma, Vishnu, and Rudra, but of all three at the same time. This Kaula path of Pada Uttistha is knowledge concerning the non-Self. This privileged knowing allows one to become like the god of love, independent and fully realized. O Kaula Devi, the true doctrine of knowledge is thus declared. It is stationed in the throat.

PATALA 14

$\mathcal{T}$he meditation on the throat center is allied with the central channel, in which the wheels will manifest freely depending on the practice, the moment, the season, the heat, the cold, and the surrounding colors. Yoga is one. It is unified with nature. It amounts to becoming an element of nature once again, a brother of the trees, of the earth, of the sky, of the rivers, of plants. Leave behind our human pretension of negating awareness of everything that isn't us. Practice and ecstatic moments make you see clearly that you are this particle of dust that shines for an instant in a ray of sunlight. See that you are each atom, that you are the whole, the totality submerged in Shakti manifesting in the bindu. The image of the drop is very beautiful because it is undivided. There is nothing positive or negative in a drop of dew shining in the morning with the first rays of the sun. There is neither masculine nor feminine, neither Shiva nor Shakti. The bindu is the silent point that swallows all dichotomies. It is also vikalpa, the interstitial void.

The wheel of the throat is in movement. Sometimes you will feel it in the little hollow at the base of the throat between the two collarbones and sometimes you will feel it just under the frenum of the tongue and in the whole of the windpipe. Always avoid assigning an arbitrary placement to the wheels. Consider them as divinities to whom you are offering a space in your body so they can settle where they feel is best. The other day, you asked me to specify where the heart center resides, and I touched your lingam as an answer. I wanted to delocalize the heart center and have you understand that it is also found in your hands, in your feet, in your mouth, in the center of the chest. Subtle things cannot obey a static order, and the most marvelous texts, if applied with rigid literalness, give rise to great confusion. Always remember that I am teaching you the way of Shakti, the way of the yoginis: intuition, circles of influence, grace, deep lightness of touch, playfulness, uncertainty, listening to the world, crazy wisdom.

When the wheels are free to travel about in you, they will begin to appear. For as long as you force them to take up a position in an assigned spot, they will not appear.

So, sense your windpipe and let things happen. All the sacred sites of India are in you as well as the fifty sacred sites that are pieces of Shakti's dismembered body. If you integrate that, you immediately feel your body come back together.

Until we have a clear vision of the whole, our body is only fragments. Each time I touch you, I unite you with the whole, the totality.

Feel the Goddess in your windpipe!

Sweating Milk

After forming the rasa above the head, one should sprinkle it all over one's whole body. My Very Dear One, he who assiduously puts this exercise into practice is able to destroy objects in a muhurta. In an instant, one is freed from illness, affliction, death, and fever. Illnesses are destroyed just as a stag is killed by the lion. In an instant, a disease like leprosy is wiped out. Mahadevi! By using beautiful sweating, one can halt aging. A person becomes immortal by engaging in "sweating milk."

PATALA 14

This practice is a way of becoming aware that the cosmos flows through us continuously. This is presented by Matsyendranath in the form of light, of moon milk, of orgasmic pleasuring, and adamantine rivers. Because these forms move through our bodies from top to bottom, and because they are refined in space through the pores of the skin, we are given the experience that our bodies are infinitely extendible as a function of our sensitivity in the moment. It's an infinite fluctuation. And a state that most human beings feel only when they are in love, but the yoga that I'm teaching you is that of a perpetual state of being in love that needs no external object because it is whole, a totality.

Matsyendranath often speaks of vanquishing death, which should be understood as opening totally to life. When you are totally alive, there is no death.

PRACTICE 29

Breathing and the Nose Chakra

One should constrain consciousness to remain in a chakra by concentrating the breathing on the nose chakra.

PATALA 14

One of the simplest practices that my master taught children is to feel the air gently entering the nostrils and filling the body as if it were water infusing one's cells.

This is the first way of feeling the breath and uniting with it.

It is said as well that this very simple practice, accessible to everyone, opens a bridge that connects the base of the nose to the palate and releases a flow of amrita. The sense of smell develops with practice. You will smell perfumes that are farther and farther away, and this deep sensing of the perfumes of the world will make you salivate until divine amrita appears, nourishing you.

PRACTICE 30

The World in Oneself

The ten million celestial chariots (stars), the planets, the macrocosm, all movement, the Three Worlds with their inhabitants, animate beings and inanimate objects—all these are perceived as having their abode in the human body. Through constant and assiduous meditation, one can perceive this inside oneself.

PATALA 14

*J*n the sexual celebration, the two adepts having become Shiva/Shakti, they proceed, with the help of a mantra, to make their bodies sacred in order to place the fifty *pithas,* or sacred locations of India, on their bodies.

PREPARATION OF THE PLACE OF RITUAL ACCORDING TO KAULA:

Purify the place by shouting three times "KLIM PHAT!" Draw a mandala with vermilion, with sandalwood, or with water on the altar where Kali, the queen of Kaula, resides.

A square beginning with the upper right corner.

A triangle in the square.

Settle yourself in the center of the triangle with its point in front of you.

Call the guru by his Kaula name.

Call the lineage.
Call the red yoginis from the great practice.

Enter the spontaneous, nondual state of meditation, facing the Kaulika who is to be initiated. Whisper in his ear his initiation name, which includes one of the 100 names of Kali or of Tripura followed by *anandabhairava* (man) or *anandabhairavi* (woman).

The Mantras of the Planets

With the tattva mudra touch the various parts of the body:

AIM HRIM SHRIM AM AM IM IM to Aries
  (right foot).
AIM HRIM SHRIM UM UM to Taurus
  (right side of genitals).
AIM HRIM SHRIM RM RM LM LM to Gemini
  (right belly).
AIM HRIM SHRIM EM AIM to Cancer
  (right side of heart).
AIM HRIM SHRIM OM AUM to Leo
  (right shoulder).
AIM HRIM SHRIM AM AH SHHM SHAM HAM LAM
  to Virgo (right side of head).
AIM HRIM SHRIM KAM KAHM GAM GHAM NAM
  to Libra (left side of head).
AIM HRIM SHRIM CHAM CCHAM JAM JHAM NAM
  to Scorpio (left shoulder).
AIM HRIM SHRIM TAM THAM DAM DHAM
  to Sagittarius (left side of heart).
AIM HRIM SHRIM TAM THAM DAM DHAN
  to Capricorn (left side of belly).

AIM HRIM SHRIM PAM PHAM BAM BHAM MAM
    to Aquarius (left side of genitals).
AIM HRIM SHRIM YAM RAM LAM VAM KSHAM
    to Pisces (left foot).

Installation of the pithas

Installation of the sacred locations corresponding to the places where the dismembered parts of Shakti's body fell (pithas).

AIM HRIM SHRIM AM KAMARUPA head
AIM HRIM SHRIM AM VARANASI face
AIM HRIM SHRIM IM NEPAL right eye
AIM HRIM SHRIM IM PAUDRARDHANA left eye
AIM HRIM SHRIM UM PURASTHIRA KASHMIR right ear
AIM HRIM SHRIM UM KANYAKUBJA left ear
AIM HRIM SHRIM RM PURNASHEILA right nostril
AIM HRIM SHRIM RM ARBUDACHALA left nostril
AIM HRIM SHRIM RM AMRITAKHESHVARA right cheek
AIM HRIM SHRIM LM EKAMRAYA left cheek
AIM HRIM SHRIM EM TRISROTASI upper lip
AIM HRIM SHRIM AIM KAMAKOLI lower lip
AIM HRIM SHRIM OM KAILASH upper teeth
AIM HRIM SHRIM AUM BRIGUNAGARA lower teeth
AIM HRIM SHRIM AM KHEDARA tip of the tongue
AIM HRIM SHRIM AH CHANDRA PUSHKAR throat
AIM HRIM SHRIM KAM SHIRUPA right shoulder joint
AIM HRIM SHRIM KHAM OMKHARA right shoulder
AIM HRIM SHRIM GAM JALANDHARA right fist
AIM HRIM SHRIM GHAM HIMALAYA roots of right fingers
AIM HRIM SHRIM NAM KULANTHAKA tips of right fingers
AIM HRIM SHRIM CHAM DEVIKOTA right shoulder joint

AIM HRIM SHRIM CCHAM GOKARNA left shoulder

AIM HRIM SHRIM JAM MARUTESHVARA left fist

AIM HRIM SHRIM JHAM ATTAHASA roots of left fingers

AIM HRIM SHRIM NAM VIRAJA tips of left fingers

AIM HRIM SHRIM TAM RAJAGEHA right leg joint

AIM HRIM SHRIM THAM MAHAPATHA right knee

AIM HRIM SHRIM DAM KOLAPURA right ankle

AIM HRIM SHRIM DHAM ELAPURA sole of right foot

AIM HRIM SHRIM NAM KOLESVARA big toe of right foot

AIM HRIM SHRIM TAM JAYANTIKA left leg joint

AIM HRIM SHRIM THAM UJAYINI left knee

AIM HRIM SHRIM DAM CHITRA left ankle

AIM HRIM SHRIM DHAM KSHIRIKA sole of left foot

AIM HRIM SHRIM NAM HASTINAPURA big toe of left foot

AIM HRIM SHRIM PAM UDISHA right side of body

AIM HRIM SHRIM PHAM PRAYAG left side of body

AIM HRIM SHRIM BAM SHATHISHA back

AIM HRIM SHRIM BHAM MAYAPURI navel

AIM HRIM SHRIM MAM JALESHA belly

AIM HRIM SHRIM YAM MALAYA heart

AIM HRIM SHRIM RAM SHRI SHAILA right shoulder

AIM HRIM SHRIM LAM MERU nape of the neck

AIM HRIM SHRIM VAM GIRIVARA left shoulder

AIM HRIM SHRIM SHAM MAHENDRA heart in the
    center of right palm

AIM HRIM SHRIM SHAM VAMANA heart in the center
    of left palm

AIM HRIM SHRIM SAM HIRANYAPURA heart in the
    center of the sole of the right foot

AIM HRIM SHRIM HAM MAHALASHMIPURA heart in
    the center of the sole of the left foot

AIM HRIM SHRIM LAM ODDYANA from the heart to
  the genitals
AIM HRIM SHRIM KSHAM CHAYACHATRA from the
  heart to the top of the head

Place the eight chakras on the body following Matsyendranath.
Proceed to the sacred Kaula union of the Bhairava chakra.

Meditation

The two Kaulikas must meditate respectively on Anandabhairava
and Anandabhairavi, full of life and youthfulness, luminous, faces
radiant like a full moon, and in amorous union floating in night-
blue space, *mixing their essences in continuous quivering.*

Mantra

  Om anandabhairavaya namah! (Repeat 108 times)
  Om anandabhairaviya namah! (Repeat 108 times)

Sanctify the wine

  Am hrim krom svaha! (3 times)

Union

In order to carry out the Kaula ritual, Shiva and Kali must be
united through the ritual of sacred union.

The partners can be *Pûjya* (object of worship) or *Bhogya*
(partner of sexual worship). The ritual is the same followed by a
visualization of union in the first case and an actual union in the
second case. In both cases, the sacred union can be valid only during the ceremony of the Sacred Circle or for a longer duration.

For Matsyendranath, this movement of worship includes all
beings without distinction: women can be yoginis, partners, dis-

ciples, or untouchables. There is no restriction in the Kaula Way because every woman is the Goddess just as every man is Shiva.

Once the ritual has been experienced, Shiva/Kali unite freely so long as they are in a nondual state. Kali's body becomes the collection of sacred locations, and the Kaulika who bathes in it simultaneously enters those locations. Amrita, the ambrosia of the Kaulikas, is the sublime essence of Shakti, taken in at the source. Amrita is also the lunar essence visualized in the secret chakra; it bathes the yogi with lunar milk in Matsyendranath's yoga.

The Tripura mantra that seals the sacred union

Aim klim sauh tripurayai namah!

Make this Shakti (this Shiva) mine

Make this Shakti pure

Make her mine (3 times)

They drink wine to consecrate the Kaula union

Amorous union visualized or real

Hrim Devesi May her yoni (his lingam) emit floods of
  sublime essence!

Sauh Into the yoni (lingam)

Om aim klim sauh shrim hrim path svaha!

Om hsaum vim vim vim vim

Oh! Woman of knowledge!

Oh! Lunar milk!

Come to orgasm! Come profusely!

PRACTICE 31

Not Water, Not Fire, Not Earth, Not Air, Not Ether

Let us meditate on ourselves as being not water, not fire, not earth, not air, not ether; as not being above or below or in the middle; as something that is not mineral, not vegetable, or animal. This is done by situating oneself in the unmani state of mind. After meditating on himself as being empty and not empty, freed of all thought, without any movement, the wise man becomes as big as a village. Balanced by this act, he obtains many other things besides. When the jiva is dissolved in this state, he perceives inner sounds such as those emitted by the drum, the conch, the tabla, the vina, or a buzzing. Meditate on this most high state.

PATALA 14

This practice is very interesting because it is much more abstract, less magical, but especially effective in the feeling that in being nothing we are everything. And the precious point is to understand that when we are nothing, the inner dialogue dies down and gives way to silence, and in that silence sounds emerge spontaneously, music unfurls. The music of the cosmos is very delicate, very powerful. You perceive it when the ear of the heart opens.

The Colored Spheres

Blossoming within sahaja, *there dwells a tattva, which is a pure precious stone like a pearl or a firefly. This tattva is as bright as a star and flourishes in the navel center, emitting rays that are white, red, yellow, violet, and black. It is the cause of both creation and dissolution when it takes on the appearance of a being and when it melts into nothing as it is devoid of both Kula and Akula.*

PATALA 14

$\mathcal{H}$ ere we enter into the domain of colored spheres that appear when the body is vibrating space. A stanza of the *Vijnanabhairava Tantra* makes allusion to these spheres: "Consider the entire universe as if it were dissolving into more and more subtle forms until it fuses with pure consciousness."* If you reverse the meaning of the stanza, you will understand that pure consciousness is manifesting in the form of spheres. The spheres are in you and all around you. They appear in ecstatic moments when your closed eyes are turned upward or when you are seated like a tiger, your head turned skyward. The spheres can be of all sizes. Minuscule, they surround objects such as precious stones or they are like drops of dew inhabited by rainbows. In the beginning you will perceive them rather easily on plants, on the leaves

---

*Odier, trans., *Tantra Yoga,* 20.

of trees, but finally you will see them on stones and rocks. The colored spheres show you the true nature of the real—colored atoms floating in a night-blue sky. The reason why almost all of Matsyendranath's practices must be done in the night-blue sky is that it induces a contrast that reveals the subtle world that the yogi is entering. The rainbow is always present to those who have opened the eye of the heart.

The Bhairavi energy is in me. It is that energy that will initiate you into the spheres and into the rainbow body. At a certain depth of practice, visions of the natural state of mind will manifest in you. Rising up from the depths of the silent mind that is returning to the mother, to the uterus of Bhairavi from the heart/mind, the visions will manifest during non-meditation. They will resemble the practice of the *Vijnanabhairava Tantra* that you love so much, the one in which you gaze at the colored circles of the peacock's feather. *"Imagine the five colored circles of a peacock feather as being the five senses spread through limitless space and residing in the spatiality of your own heart."**

As I told you before: "The heart is the seat of the natural state. Visions and rainbows spring forth and manifest your body in a dimension of spatiality. The natural [Mahamudra] state is the union of appearances and space. The heart is the source of all things; coming back to it is mystical accomplishment. There is nothing to be found outside of it. Even in moments of turmoil, always come back to your source. The heart is also the chamber of love in which we always find ourselves again, beyond limits of space and time. Your heart is my heart. You find yourself in me and I find myself in you. No thing and no one will be able to disturb this sacred union. Bhairava and Bhairavi!"

---

*Odier, *Tantra Yoga,* 17.

Retreating into total darkness is favorable for the development of visions of the spheres. They can roll over your body like drops of nectar, they can form a cloak of light, they can carry you into space, and can make you disappear into them. You can become immense or tiny like a drop of water with five colors.

Don't ever fixate on these visions. They come and go, never reproducing the same forms. They are the play of vibration, of spanda. Sometimes, when the apparitions become familiar, they appear during activities, in the light of day; sometimes they offer you the vision of the infinite structure of all things, the cosmic dance of atoms and of matter. You see this dance in plants, in minerals, in animals, and in human beings when they recognize their absolute essence. The visions are the prelude to rainbow body practice.

Inside the body, the first sphere often emerges in the wheel of the navel and from there spreads through the body where it dances and impregnates the real. It's like a pollination of flowers by the red goddesses in the form of bees.

As always, when the visions spring forth, it is important to not become attached to them by trying to make them happen again. Be like the sky where a rainbow never appears the same way twice. Everything arises spontaneously when you have offered your body to space.

PRACTICE 33

The Worship of Devi

At night, the adept should worship Devi. At the center of two sugar canes . . . within resides the Supreme Devi, the cause and creator of both the animate and the inanimate. Everything dissolves in her yoni nadi. In making use of this stable doctrine, one becomes attached to neither merit nor fault.

PATALA 14

*W*orship of the goddess who appears before you in night-blue space is essential. Worshipping her means you become Her. Her yoni nadi is so welcoming that she offers you to reside there in love. It's not only an image; in this contemplation, she becomes reality. The central channel of the woman is naturally open. The guru transmits secret teachings to her so that she transmits them to men.

You imagine the goddess above you in space.

The tide of ambrosia that pours from her yoni flows onto your fontanel and causes memories of birth to arise in you. Every human being emerges from Shakti.

Here, you are going to return to the place of your creation.

Imagine that the yoni of the goddess opens wide and slowly sucks you in.

Your head approaches the yoni. You smell her marvelous

orgasmic juices that flow over your face. You delight in the marvelous savor and in the divine taste of amrita.

Little by little, the lips of the goddess's yoni caress and suck
in your head. The whole bony structure of your skull begins to
tremble, to soften until the moment when your whole head slips
inside the yoni of the goddess.

Then, your whole body returns to the place of its creation.

You curl up in this divine warmth.

You curl up in me.

You are me!

PRACTICE 34

Orgasmic Pleasuring
and the Wheels

Thanks to his knowledge of the nature of Kula, and by being established in the Kula, the master of the supreme tattva on the Kulayana path can arouse sexual ecstasy with the vajra reed. In taking one's leave from gurus, siddhas, and devatas, that which is white as the Moon should flow into the sea of milk.

PATALA 14

*I*n this return to sexual practice, still couched in twilight language, there is the explanation of another practice where the sperm flows into the sea of milk of Shakti.

You need to understand that there are two sorts of flow—one upward and the other downward. They don't contradict each other and indicate two moments of sexual worship. First, the breath directs the sperm upward where it nourishes the wheels and doesn't flow away. Then, after infinite Shiva-Shakti games, it flows out into Shakti's sea of milk.

It's not a question of control, but of breathing, and the breath can play with the essence of the orgasmic pleasuring by distributing it through the whole body and the whole cosmos, then making it an offering to Shakti.

This secret of the yogini's Kaula is bestowed by grace and through the breath. It is this deep yoga that is revealed to beings whose hearts are grand.

The Skulls Practice

Visualize skulls at the tips of the fingernails. In a similar way, one should visualize them inside the center of the chakra of the bones. This Sahaja chakra is known to be a powerful vajra. A man becomes a vajra by practicing Vajra yoga. Above a marvelous chakra with one thousand koti petals, there is another lotus with seven thousand million petals and filaments. Being surrounded three times with milk inside this lotus, one must force one's body to bathe in this milk.

PATALA 15

The skulls are a reference to Kalika and her collar of fifty skulls symbolizing the gyration of the fifty Sanskrit letters around Kali's neck. In our case, there are twenty skulls: sacred texts emerge, flowing from your body through your fingers and toes. In the Tandava dance, imagine that you are distributing basic texts as trails of light in the cosmos. This also means that your whole skeleton, your structure, is inhabited by texts, mantras, and mudras.

There is no longer anything outside you.

All the stanzas of these texts are continually traveling about in you.

By touching feet and hands, one touches the essence of the teachings.

PRACTICE 36

Kaliki Yogini

Kaliki Yogini is famous everywhere. I obtained this Akula by making a pilgrimage and, at the end of this kalpa or yuga, it has remained within me. It dwells in the heart of jiva, inseparable just as the fruit and flowers are inseparable from the roots of a plant, or just as the leaves and branches belong to a tree. O Kulabhamini! It resides in my body. Those who don't know about it are pashus. After having recovered this famous, grand knowledge for the second time, it was offered to you—to you, to Kameshi, to Skanda, to Gana, to Nandi, to Mahakali, to Jaya, to Vijaya, to Bhatta, to Dronaka, and finally to Hara Siddhika. The characteristics of Kaula were explained to a yogi by Kalika. From Mahakaula came the Siddha Kaula, and from the Siddha Kaula it was transmitted to Matsyendra.

PATALA 16

This lineage of the Kaula practice takes it marvelously all the way back to Kali. This is how we come to see the presence of darkness as a jewel box for light and as a ferment of illumination. This presence also marks the coming together of violence and absolute love—a single sphere in which all opposites are done away with.

The Subtle Centers

This great yoga stresses that the breath of life is stationed in the centers of the anus, of the genitals, of the navel, of the heart, of the lotus of the great uvula, of the ghantika wherein are the granthis and the "great white place," of the base of the nose at the dvadashanta, in-between the eyebrows, on the forehead, at the Brahmarandhra, and at the shikha. In this way the eleven subtle centers are shown. They are known to reside in the body's central axis.

PATALA 17

The subtle centers, the wheels, being a descending and ascending movement of energy, become established spontaneously. The practices are only an invitation to manifest them. Any tension, any trying to feel them, only grinds things to a halt. Kaula yoga is a total handing over of the body to divine space.

PRACTICE 38

Vatuka, Protector of the Teachings

One must meditate on Vatuka who is wearing red clothing, holding a staff, and has matted hair. He is as luminous as Brahma, the destroyer of obstacles. Hrim Vatuka—one must recite this vidya when suffering from a great anxiety.

Patala 16

*V*atuka is a very dynamic form of Bhairava energy. His body radiates like a clear ruby. Vatuka is the protector of the teaching and of the Kaulikas.

You float naked in night-blue space and you let Vatuka emerge in the center of your heart. He looks like a yogi—young and flamboyant, with long hair piled on his head. There are feminine aspects to his body and his energy. Seated in the center of your heart, he dominates and sees everything moving through your body. He immediately chases away all thought, all fear, all hesitation that could prevent you from merging with all that is. Armed with a staff, he chases away all contradictory or dual elements in your body. You hear the whistling of Vatuka's staff and you identify with him by saying his mantra inwardly: *Hrim ca Vatuka hrim.*

Since sacred places have been established in your body thanks to my touch, Vatuka is the protector of these sacred places in you. His joyful youthfulness makes him particularly lively. Call on him in hard times—he will make room right away.

PRACTICE 39

The Music of the Infinite Body

In listening to the inner sound of the heart, one can know the qualities of Hamsa. *In the throat chakra, this celestial sound, dhvani, has Kalas, the nature of which is cause and effect. Above the last underworld, it (Hamsa) is called Vama, having been wrapped from above and invested with form. From a point near the anus, it rises up until it is absorbed once more in the dvadashanta. Thus,* Hamsa *moves around in the centers of the body, being neither good nor bad, stainless, lacking an organ, celestial, pure, very subtle, transparent, unified, eternal, blissful, giving birth yet free from birth.*

PATALA 17

One of the most surprising things, when you are immersed in the Kaula Way practices, is the arising of inner sound and its clear perception. The music of the yogi's body goes hand in hand with his delicious perfume. In complete solitude one often hears external songs like wind on rocks or in trees, the murmuring of brooks, the clamor of waterfalls, birds seen or not seen, the fineness of the songs of night birds, the stridulations of insects in summer, the humming butterfly wings, the hissing of snakes, and the cries of wolves and tigers. All of that populates the apparent solitude of ascetics whose sensitivity opens to the music of life.

But the day comes when, in the silence preceding dawn, at the Bhairava hour, inner music suddenly wells up. But rare are those who perceive it. You have to begin by refining your sensitivity in listening to the world. This is the role of the *Hamsa* mantra that flourishes on the breath. There's a silence that gives birth to music.

PRACTICE 40

The Yoga of Looking with Your Skin

All of Devi's limbs in the chakra are very radiant and have heavenly forms. In practicing, the adept finds himself in the center of these sixteen petals. When one is seeking liberation, one should meditate on the auspicious devis who are dressed in white. When one desires the presence of the siddhi yoginis, one should meditate on them as being black-skinned, young, maidenly, wearing red clothing, smeared with blood, wearing red ornaments, adorned with flowers and red garlands. Each one of them should be worshipped as united with oneself. When one wants something, one should meditate mentally on Shri Natha coupled with his yogini who is holding a conch and is surrounded by hosts of subtle forms.

PATALA 19

*T*he red goddesses do nothing but dance within you. Through this beautiful practice they also reveal to you the marmas—energy points—that are distributed throughout the body. This practice brings in a slippage of the senses from one arbitrarily assigned domain into another domain. For example, you become able to taste a sound or touch an image produced from your mind. This is a very important practice because a great deal of our mental partitioning and our conditioning is founded on the immutability of our sensory system. When each sense has its own exclusive domain, we are maintained in an arbitrary cohesion that yoga brings into question, allowing us to experience all kinds of other possibilities. This is the foundation of poetry and the perception of the spatiality of all things.

You are floating naked in night-blue space.

In space, twenty red goddesses appear. They dance the Tandava around you in exuberant joy.

One of them places herself on your fontanel and immediately her body transforms into a sparkling ruby.

Another goddess places herself on your center between the eyebrows and transforms into a sparkling ruby.

Two red goddesses place themselves in your eyes and transform into rubies.

A goddess places herself on the tip of your tongue.

A goddess in the cavity at the base of the throat.

Two goddesses at the points under your clavicle where the shoulder is rounded.

Concentrate on these first eight points and feel deeply that they are connected to one another by very fine and very brilliant rays of red light.

Now, starting from the shoulder points, imagine that two goddesses fly through your body, leaving a sparkling red wake that turns into a beautiful ruby on the tip of your coccyx. From this moment forward, it may happen that your body begins to vibrate. A goddess traces a luminous ray and places herself in your anus, as Matsyendranath tells us in Patala 17.

Another goddess flies toward the tip of your lingam or your clitoris depending on whether you are projecting yourself as a man or as a woman. Try to feel deeply the whole circuit right up to the fontanel. Kali is often represented with an eye on her clitoris.

Two red goddesses fly through your legs to your big toes. Then, when the luminous circuit is established, they fly again to the clitoris or the tip of the lingam and from there they continue on to the two points to the right and to the left of the navel.

They melt down their energies and fly toward the heart center, leaving rays of red light behind them.

They divide up once again in order to touch your nipples.

They reunite in order to touch the throat point.

Then the tip of the tongue.

Then the two eyes.

Then the center between the eyebrows.

They then hurry on to the fontanel, which closes the circuit of the primary marmas. At this moment you can feel a discharge arising from the connection among the energy points.

You visualize your body as it becomes luminous in night-blue space, until you see only the red points and the circuit that connects them.

Now the twenty rubies transform into eyes.

You can see the whole night-blue space around you.

Remain in this contemplation . . .

From each eye, dozens of little eyes appear, rolling around on your skin until all of your skin is looking. You see everything in all its brilliance.

Imagine now that all these eyes begin to flow back into your two physical eyes. The power of your look is now charged with the total depth of the marmas.

Now open your eyes and look at the part of my body or my clothing that you had chosen before beginning. See the richness and the depth of each fiber of the cotton cloth, the luminous density, the light of the fibers that weave together.

Now look at the forest, the trunks of trees and leaves. Dive into the extreme richness of the real.

Let's go see the colored mosses, the earth in all its granular detail!

The red goddesses can be dancing or sometimes they can present themselves in the form of rubies as in this practice. You are floating in night-blue space. Opposite you, in the distance, a sparkling ruby appears. You contemplate it, fascinated. Little by little, the ruby approaches you near your navel.

You feel its emanation and its heat.

It positions itself on your navel and irradiates the interior of your body.

With a deep breath in, you pull the ruby into your body and, as soon as it has entered, it roams around inside you leaving behind a red wake.

The more the ruby explores inside your body, the more your body becomes colored with its marvelous light. Your bones, your organs, your muscles melt into the red.

The ruby gives birth to other rubies. All these moving rubies fill your body until you become a red, quivering mass, an expression of spanda.

At that moment you breathe out deeply, then breathe in slowly.

You breathe out again, a little more deeply; then you breathe in a little more.

You breathe out once more, all the way so there isn't the slightest breath left in you. You pause for two or three seconds followed by a very big in-breath, at the climax of which you imagine that your body bursts into thousands of red particles, exploding in the night-blue sky to form stars and galaxies.

PRACTICE 41

Worship of the Kaula Shakti

Now I will explain the characteristics of the vira and his Shakti. She is the ultimate one with eyes of dazzling white. She is a devi with disheveled hair, very beautiful and eloquent, her ten arms radiating outward. She is devoted to Kula and worships the devi of the guru. She is beautiful, joyful, and has a perfect countenance with nice eyebrows. She devotes herself to the Kulagama, free of all fear, very calm, exquisitely fine in nature, expresses herself with truth, free from the slightest doubt. She knows nothing of cruelty. She is a devi with a perfect body, aware of her beautiful appearance like the heroine who is the Shakti of Rudra—the "Root Devata." He who, having learned of the origin and the location of the Maha Lingam, the stem of the flower in flames, can become like the bindu. The unalterable Shakti of all the Shaktis is the internal Shakti of the atma. After becoming aware of this Shakti who originates in one's body, one can unite with her.

PATALA 20

*T*he marvelous Shakti manifests in the body of a yogini or a yogi. She protects him and transmits the teaching to him. Venerating her reveals everything that has to be revealed!

This Shakti is also pure presence, barely palpable, without characteristics.

She can choose to appear in multiple forms as indicated in the next practice, which encourages worship of the feminine in all its forms.

In Sadhana there are moments when we need materiality and incarnation to leave behind the armor that makes us deaf to the totality. There are other moments in which union is so integrated that it comes together in pure presence within us. It is then no longer a question of unifying or not unifying. All is one.

PRACTICE 42

Shakti's Animal Forms

"How do the Kaula yoginis move about on the Earth, O Deva?"

Bhairava says: "In the world of mortals, all the devatas can move around there. Hear me! They exist as female turtledoves, vultures, swans, and as hens and other birds; also as female dogs, wolves, owls, falcons, bees or beetles, jackals, sheep, buffalo, cats, camels, mongooses, tigers, timid elephants, peacocks, and cuckoos. In various other female forms, the yoginis can live on Earth. It is imperative to venerate these forms and the yoginis delight in them. Merciful Kuleshvari: When they die, they should not be eaten. They also exist as horses, cocks, snakes, stags, and some who appear as human beings or appear as scorpions, bulls, mice, or frogs. We can be perturbed by the planets, bhutas, flames, fires, swords, difficult situations, obstructions, disease, kings, lightning, tigers, lions, or elephants. Additionally, we can be under the influence of various anxieties, causing things to appear from any direction. In this case, we must seek the protection of the sixty-four yoginis who wander in various forms by taking on the appearance of various animals. We must never say or think anything arising from anger toward these forms. In the same way, we must never speak harshly to maidens or women. We worship women and maidens because they represent Shakti placed under Kula protection."

PATALA 23

*T*he power of the sixty-four yoginis is found in every feminine element, be it vegetable, animal, mineral, or human. From its initial origin onward, the practice of the Kaula Way, as transmitted by the yoginis, brings about an alchemical transmutation of the body, which then becomes the receptacle of the feminine nature of all things. This is an extremely important point. Without this respect and this worship of the feminine and of women, consciousness will never manage to emerge from the dynamic of the pashu—someone common, vulgar.

The worry being raised here can happen at any moment and the being who is not connected to the feminine will be swallowed up by the chaotic energies of the Kali Yuga.

Identifying with the cosmos is the end of loneliness!

PRACTICE 43

The Dance of the Red Yoginis

The Kula siddhas, the yoginis, the Rudras, and the Devi chakra all dwell in the head and heart centers. My Dear One! Listen to the rules of the external puja. One offers a sweet perfume, camphor, garlands of beautiful flowers, champaka blossoms, sweet-scented blue lotuses, red blossoms, a diversity of one hundred different flowers, tree resins mixed with honey, meat tambula, soma, incense, sandalwood, aloe wood, musk, very red flowers, fragrant kinds of incense and flames. Flowers devoid of scent are terrible and should not be presented as offerings. The external puja has been explained. Listen now concerning the meditation. All the yoginis will be dressed in red and their faces will be coated with red paste. They must make up a group of sixteen having sweet faces and adorned with jewels. They will drink a liquor distilled from madira flowers. Like Iccha, each one of them is freed from fever and death. Each one of them will be the cause of creation and will grant her own favors. He who meditates on them will live long.

PATALA 24

$\mathcal{I}$n this final practice, Matsyendranath provides a beautiful introduction to the worship of the red yoginis, but he remains silent about the second part of the ritual because it involves sexual practices that must be carefully hidden. He hints at it, however, in the second-to-last sentence. Here is the ritual in its mental form:

You are floating in night-blue space, but this time you are dancing the Tandava. Naked and using the "Hra Hro" mantra you call the yoginis to come dance with you. You offer them garlands of fragrant flowers, honey, sandalwood, musk, alcohol, food, or more simply, since it is an internal puja, you offer your own heart. In the Kaula Way, external practice is almost never used—everything is done using intense imagination but there are of course exceptions. Sometimes we take a ritual bath in the waterfall!

The sixteen yoginis appear, one after the other. Their energy is quite joyful and crazy in this practice. They are not at all threatening. Your body becomes more and more luminous. The yoginis are peaceful at the moment. They are undulating languorously, but they are not yet dancing the Tandava. They are watching you dance. They are waiting for your body's light to become even more adamantine. A sixteen-petalled lotus appears in your heart center and as your skin has become diaphanous, open, hardly different from the space that surrounds you, the yoginis approach slowly. They caress your skin as if finding their way into you. They literally open you up and slip into you. Each of them sits down on one of the petals of the lotus. They undulate gently in time with the first rhythm of the dance. Their bodies absorb the offerings, the clothes, the sandalwood paste, and their red nakedness is revealed to you. They are beautiful, transparent like liquid ruby. You continue to dance in night-blue space and you match your rhythm to the subtle slowness of the yoginis, like musicians preparing to play together.

The sixteen red yoginis begin to let their arms explore your inner space, which plunges you into quivering, into spanda. They caress the inside of your skin and the almost invisible shadows of your organs. They are floating in you, just as you are floating in night-blue space.

On each petal the yoginis rise up and begin to dance. Your whole body is activated and vivified by their presence.

The dance of the yoginis becomes progressively more passionate and you follow their beat, their rhythm.

Suddenly, the yoginis jump into your body leaving the lotus petals behind. They occupy your whole body with their wildly rhythmic dance, and you feel your body expand into space to provide them with a bigger field of action.

As your body expands, the movements of the yoginis become larger and faster. In studying their faces, you realize that mystic ecstasy and erotic ecstasy have come together and you see their luminous orgasmic pleasuring flow along their thighs while you gather it up at its source with your tongue and your face, moving from one yogini to the other in a crazy erotic dance where they give themselves to you until you become infinite space.

There is one sentence that contains the whole essence of the practice explained in the *Kaulajnananirnaya Tantra:*

"The way is to act according to one's own will, while being aware of both the Akula and the Kula of Devi."

PART II

The
Kaulajnananirnaya Tantra

The *Kaulajnananirnaya Tantra*
was Translated from the Sanskrit by
Dominique Boubouleix.*

*I know of no Dharmma superior to that of the Kaulas,
by adherence to which man becomes possessed of Divine
knowledge. I am telling Thee the truth, O Devi! Lay it to the
heart and ponder over it. There is no doctrine superior to the
Kaulika doctrine, the most excellent of all. This is the most
excellent path kept hidden by reason of the crowd of Pashus,
but when the Kali Age advances this pathway will be revealed.*

MAHANIRVANA TANTRA, IV, 43–45[†]

*Boubouleix's French text is here translated into English by Jack Cain.
†*Tantra of the Great Liberation (Mahānirvāna Tantra)*, trans. Arthur Avalon
[John Woodroffe] (London: Luzac, 1913).

❖ Patala One ❖

From the tips of the big toes emanate the tattvas. In the Kula sphere, O Devi, Knowledge is divided into eighteen categories. In this way, O Bhairavi, the process of creation itself is announced. What else do you want to hear? What has been kept secret is now revealed.

✤ Patala Two ✤

Devi says: "The heat of five fires is equal to the heat of millions of millions of suns. This heat has now been explained entirely by Your Grace, O Bhairava! The process of creation will now be known to me. Speak to me at present about the dissolution of the Cosmos."

Bhairava says: "I will explain to you how dissolution comes about. The fire known as Kalagnirudra is eternally situated in the tip of the nail of the big toe. When it flames upward, then dissolution is set in motion. It resides in the mouth of the 'sea horse' (*badava*), at the heart of deepest subterranean world. There exist seven subterranean worlds situated under heaven. This is how the fourteen worlds manifest, O Merciful One. One needs to know that the form of the ultimate tattva is located in the center of the body, O Omniscient One, both dissolution and that which is reabsorbed into the sphere of Shakti. Shakti dissolves into Shiva. Shiva dissolves into Kriya, action. Kriya is reabsorbed into Jnana, knowledge. Jnana dissolves into Iccha, desire. The fire of the Supreme Shakti resides in the place where the Shakti of Iccha is reabsorbed. I have declared to you the characteristics of dissolution, O My Beautiful One. The universe absorbs Kruddha, rage, which constitutes half the dissolution. The other half is represented by the very process of creation, the manifestation of the moving and of the fixed. O Varanane! Pleasure is inferior and liberation is superior. Devi, I have previously stated the process of creation to you. The principle of Kula is described as an alternating dissolution and creation. What else do you want to hear, O Lady, regarding what has been kept secret, but which can be now revealed?"

⁙ Patala Three ⁙

Devi says: "Great Lord, I have questions concerning the characteristics of Kula, of the Self, and of consciousness. O Shankara Natha, O you who bestow felicity, be so kind as to reply."

Bhairava says: "Listen attentively to the Kula characteristics. Where the mind resides, there dwell also the senses, the objects of the senses, and the body—they are impregnated by one's own Shakti, one's embodied being, and the five tattvas. It is said that meditation on an internal center constitutes a clear comprehension of the body. Everything proceeds from the letters of the Sanskrit alphabet, which is the dwelling place of the absolute void. My Dear One! Inside the body reside the chakras of five lines, of sixteen lines, of sixty-four petals, and the marvelous lotus of one thousand petals. Above, there is a very brilliant lotus of ten million petals. Above the lotus of ten million petals, there is a lotus of thirty million petals, each one of which has a halo identical to a flame. Above is the All in its fullness, absolute, eternal, like an immobile lotus, free and unalterable. It penetrates everything. From its very will, it is the cause of creation and dissolution. The animate and the inanimate, both of them, are dissolved in this Lingam, the phallus of Shiva. It is the sphere that penetrates everything, once again without a pot, without a container. It is necessary to understand that the fact of being in chains implies ignorance of this, whereas he who knows this becomes liberated from his chains. This sphere is devoid at one and the same time of mind and the absence of mind, freed from meditation and practice. Clearly, it is in harmony with everything because it is eternal like the blue Atasi flower. Divine essence possesses at one and the same time color and the absence of coloration, which is accomplished only thanks to knowledge and in belonging to the lineage of the succession of masters and disciples. Devi, the Kula characteristics have been stated. The lingam that is not in wood, in stone, fashioned from clay, in the form of a gem, in copper, in iron, in brass, in crystal, in tin, in lead, or in copper raises us up to the various blossomings of red flowers and it is worshipped in all worlds. Devi, one should not be concerned with the eighteen treatises, such as those of Adhyatmika and others. Mahadevi, this kind of concern comes from the pashu who is devoid of the slightest bit of knowledge. All those who advance on the path of spiritual understanding should not associate with such ignorant people, because they have strayed into useless paths, since they have been stripped of the knowledge of Kula.

Everything manifests from the center of the bindu: Brahma, all the gods and the asuras, the saints, the yakshas, the gandharvas, the siddhas, the plants, the trees, the insects, the planets, the celestial constellations, the stars and all the rest, everything that is found in the cosmos, fixed or in movement, the elements and every other thing. This lingam, the cause of creation and dissolution, is worshipped by the siddhas. It shines with its own light, being pure, eternal, entirely unlimited. It is like the flame at the end of time and like lightning in the sky. One arrives at liberation after having known this vivifying lingam. This lingam is eternally erect like a vajra lingam. There is no way it can be destroyed by the wrath of fire or by any collapse. Devi, a Kaulika should worship it in order to obtain the siddhis, the so-coveted supernatural powers, by making use of flowers of thought, incense with the most delicate scents, and other necessary objects.

The first flower (chakra) is without harmfulness; the second represents constraints of the senses; the third, generosity; the fourth, right attitude; the fifth, compassion; and the sixth, freedom from the slightest cruelty. The seventh flower symbolizes meditation and the eighth flower, knowledge. Having learned of these rules concerning the flowers, one must worship the image of this lingam in the mind. Worshipping the form of the lingam, one can obtain simultaneously freedom and joy. Devi, it is the lingam that bestows the siddhis while residing in a steady and powerful body. One should always meditate on the mental image of the lingam in order to come to the highest and most remarkable self-knowledge.

Thus, O Devi, I have declared the characteristics of the Kaulika body lingam. Any other external usage of the lingam must be abandoned, such as that of the lingams of stone, wood, or clay. The ordinary path is devoid of success and liberation. The secret meaning of everything that resides in the body belongs to the Kula Agama. Whoever interprets this as the act of placing a lingam outside himself, enters the pashu's arena. Devi, the secret meaning of this knowledge has been given to you. One must never reveal it to persons who lack devotion."

Devi says: "Now, O Lord of the Gods! Speak to me of the results that intense practice produces. By your grace, Bhairava, explain to me what is the nature of the imperishable body. How can one put an end to the supernatural aggressions premeditated by others and that affect home or country? O My Refuge! Speak to me about everything concerning interferences, about what helps attract things to oneself, about what generates eloquent images and the breaking of pots and stones."

Bhairava says: "You do well to ask me that, O Mahadevi. Therefore, I'm going to speak to you about it. One must create the Kula of the body by bringing together the apertures of the nadis, the subtle channels. The pinda consists of a vidya mantra—the knowledge mantra. It is the splendid bestower of happiness and liberation. By lighting a flame above and below the apertures of each nadi, one says 'vam' while visualizing these Sanskrit letters being the color of molten gold. Then, darkness and light will be simultaneously dissolved in the circle of birth, and the sadhaka (yogi) can enter into the body of the beast he wants. By using 'hum ho,' he can accomplish that with all fixed and mobile things simultaneously.

In meditating on Shakti as being the Bindu Nada, the drop, the sound, and in bringing together darkness and light to dissolve them in the bursting circle of birth, one must meditate on the fact that such a thing is happening in the body. In half the blink of an eye, anyone can find himself paralyzed. O Magnificent One!

One has to have meditated on Shakti and visualized her as a beautiful woman seated in the five ethers. In this way, one can paralyze the whole world instantly while making use of one of the mental abilities concerning the knowledge of Shakti. After having connected the object of one's meditation with a noose, one can then tie knots. In using the order of the nada of Parashakti, one can then tear apart someone's body, after having bound his vital energy using a mudra. At present, I will answer the question concerning visions of the past and the future.

O Bhairavi! The Kula Pinda is made up of the letters 'a' to 'ha.' Using a conch and in conducting the ritual of polishing the teeth, the lips and the whole body, one holds a flower in one's hands and one uses one letter of the Sanskrit alphabet to light the flame. Thanks to this method, one can cause the death of others, uproot, paralyze, deceive, calm, heal, attract, or subjugate. Knowing the fifty letters allows everything to be done, My Dear One! 'Hum' causes death. 'Yum yah' has the effect of moving one into the distance. 'Rum ra' causes fever. 'Vum va' facilitates studying. 'Lum la' paralyzes others. 'Shum sha' pacifies. 'Sum sa' is used to oppress others. 'Ksum ksa' helps capturing animals. 'Klim ksnim' helps subjugate others. 'Klem ksom' promotes agitation and deceives others. 'Som sa' facilitates the deployment of siddhis.

'Ho hah' destroys poisons. 'Hro hrah' attracts the red yoginis. 'Jum sa' bestows victory over death, gives rise to eloquent images, and breaks objects. 'Srom sah' blocks nooses and fosters love. 'Bhrur tra' bestows Dakini siddhis. 'Jhu ra' bestows the Rakshasi siddhis. 'Lum la' bestows the Lakini siddhis. 'Lum ka' bestows the Kusu Malini siddhis. 'Yum ya' bestows the Yogini siddhis. 'Hrim ha' fosters the attraction of others to oneself.

By separating out each bija from the group of Sanskrit letters, one can accomplish all the actions that one desires. One who is initiated should carry out the reverse Matrka and worship she who is Kula's support. Having known all, one becomes an expert having characteristics of the greatest strength. He who visualizes the beast (*pashu,* animal nature), which dissolves in the supreme lingam, which is the abode of flame, becomes independent and totally liberated. Everything that exists resides in his heart, since he knows all the qualities and is perfect like Bhairava. The teachings that you have asked me about, those that bestow the siddhis, must remain secret, O Clement One. One must carefully hide them from the wicked who are without the slightest devotion and one must not reveal them to those devoid of love. We can only reveal them to the Kaulika who wants to obtain the siddhis."

⚜ Patala Five ⚜

Devi says: "O You Who Bestow Grace, Mahadeva, speak to me freely about the way to overcome death. When that is not known, life is nothing but a wandering in ignorance on Earth. Speak to me from the whole profundity of your being, Mahadeva, about this method by which a person can walk the Earth while attaining immortality!"

Bhairava says: "By gaining knowledge of this secret doctrine and through the constant practice of meditation, free of all duality, we can achieve a very high state. Through incessant practice, we can accomplish everything that one can mentally desire, such as the following siddhis: Uttistha, stout-heartedness; Khadga, sexual power; Patala, the exploration of subterranean worlds; Rocana, satisfaction; Anjana, vision most clear; Paduka, moving around at lightning speed; Rasa, orgasmic pleasuring and all alchemical knowledge. Each person can accomplish all these things if he practices meditation this way. There is no doubt about that. My Dear One, listen with attention to the explanation of the knowledge about which I am conversing with you. We must meditate inwardly on a pure outburst of white light. This outburst must be refreshing, celestial, have a mellow scent, and it must extend off to infinity. It is the divine raison d'être of all refreshing libations of a lunar nature as well as being the center of space. It flows in us through all the many channels. By attaining that, we can have a long life and overcome death. The application of this method protects us from fever and from death; no one is ever again subject to disease or various ailments. Through this divine game, O Sweet-faced Lady, is bestowed the recompense of the siddhis. We must meditate, visualizing that in the middle of an Ocean of milk there is a great, pure lotus that is white. At the center of this lotus of 100,000,000,000 petals, the wise man visualizes his own being, while wearing white clothing and white ornaments. My Very Dear One, by meditating on the fact that we become one with this lotus, we have no need to feed ourselves! We must meditate on the rays that are white like milk while imagining that they are impregnating our minds. The rays liberate us from illness, from fever, from death, and from attachments. We can then play and enjoy ourselves in various ways, following our own will.

At present, I am going to reveal the whole doctrine specific to the victory over death. After having meditated on the dwelling place or seat of the Moon, and after having made contact with the higher Moon by meditating on the mind impregnated with the divine freshness of the lunar rays, we are liberated from fever, from death, and from all diseases. Through the application of this method over the course of one year, we will be assisted by the Kula yoginis.

Listen, O Kulabhavini Devi, to this other marvel! Meditate mentally on the Moon as being a Full Moon, entire and complete. You will never again know fever or illness. Kalyani Bhavini, now listen once again! We will meditate on the idea that this Moon resides in the navel, in the head, and in the heart. In practicing continually this way, so that we maintain ourselves constantly in a harmonious state of awareness during one year, we are completely liberated and separated from fever as well as from death. Once again, please listen carefully to this other method, O Lady Worshipped by the Viras! Meditate on the beautiful thousand-petalled lotus, which will be as white as pure cow's milk, just as if Devi was appearing in each of the chakras. In each of the chakras there flows an equal amount of lunar nectar and they are all sprinkled by the highest chakra. The yogi must continuously practice this sprinkling of his being with the nectar. He will then be liber-

ated, avoiding old age and the slightest illness. He will be able to
frolic in the ocean of samsara, My Very Dear One, for he will be
fulfilled and will attain his independence.

There is another marvel, O Devi! Listen attentively. After
having meditated on a sixteen-petalled lotus, snowy white like
the color of the Moon, each petal being a sphere for Shiva's love
games, we must visualize our own bodies bathed by the tide of
nectar that flows over them, each one of these currents looking
snowy white like the color of milk bathing our bodies and oozing from the pores. Then we will be like Shiva, no longer having
to submit to fever, having no need of food, not knowing illness
or death, completely independent, moving by our own will alone,
and being adored by 100,000,000,000 gods and by numerous
heavenly maidens. Devi, there are altogether eleven chakras plus
the thousand-petalled chakra. They are located in the genitals, the
navel, the heart, the throat, in the mouth, on the forehead, at the
top of the cranium, in the bony joints of the cranium, and inside
the Tridanda. Each one has 5, 8, 10, 12, 16, 100, and 10,000,000
petals, respectively.

Meditating on each one of the areas of the body confers various results. The color red always confers being all-powerful over
others and a great serenity. Natha and yellow cause paralysis.
Violet makes us always move far away. It is said that white ensures
good health and has us also enjoy deep peace. It is said that the
dazzling milky white color confers victory over death. With molten gold of dazzling brightness, we can make cities totter.

After having meditated on each of the chakras separately, considering that they are of a consistency similar to the original point,
the cosmic sound, and Shakti, we obtain the grace of dharma, of
artha, of kama, and of moksha, as well as anima and the eight
other siddhis. Then we can see the future and have the power to

create. There is no doubt that we can become like that through the constant practice of what has already been revealed. He who is initiated in the Kula Kaula Agama and who recites 'the conqueror of death,' O Devi, becomes, without any doubt, immortal and the guru of pious yoginis. Devi, thus we have explained to you the characteristics of the secret knowledge about the victory over death. One should very carefully conceal it in one's home in the world of mortals. This thing is hard to obtain, even for the siddhas. Therefore, keep it well hidden. One should reveal it only to disciples previously tested for more than a year."

❧ Patala Six ❧

Devi says: "Now I want to know the characteristics of jiva. In what being does jiva appear? What is the real nature of a jiva? What color is it? What is its extent? Where is it situated? How does it disappear? Speak to me of all that!"

Bhairava says: "Listen, O Viracamunda, to the characteristics of jiva. It is supreme, whole, eternal. It consists of nothing and is indestructible. It is the ultimate atomic particle, the Natha, the supreme Shiva that penetrates everything. It is the ultimate jiva. It is Hamsa, the soul of Shakti. It is the mind, the breath, the buddhi, and the citta that are found situated in the breathing in and breathing out of all living beings. When it leaves the body, it becomes supreme Shiva. According to the uninterrupted succession of masters, through oral transmission, O Devi, it resides in the navel, the heart, the mouth, and the nostrils. This is Kaulika knowledge, O Devi, which has been transmitted to us by the oral tradition. Through hearing that, by knowledge, or by meditating on that, we can liberate ourselves from everything and reach attainment. After six months of this practice, one becomes instantaneously liberated from all bonds. Leprosy, disease, and needs—all that disappears. One is then liberated from all illness and the yoginis reside in us. One is spiritualized and becomes omnipotent like a siddha who has attained anima and all the other powers. Thus I have explained to you the practice of jiva, O Bhairavi. We must reveal it to the truly devout of the Kulagama, to the gurus, to the devis, and to the sadhakas who are of good character. The quintessence of Kaulika that induces yoginis to appear must not be offered to hypocrites, to false-hearted persons, or to those who remain prisoners of the material universe."

Devi says: "O Lord of the Gods! Speak to me now of the

results and of the greatness of tapas. Please explain the knowledge concerning the nirmalya body that breaks up. A great knowledge has been revealed. It is difficult to obtain, even for the gods. Now I wish to hear from you about the illusion of time."

Bhairava says: "O Lady! What you are asking of me remains very mysterious. Without any doubt, I am speaking about what liberates us from death. We must satiate ourselves with amrita, the divine nectar, the very essence of Brahma. After a month, one can vanquish death. It is true! By placing amrita at the root of the palate, one must gradually ingest the breath of life. O Devi! After six months of diligent practice, liberation from the direst illnesses will spring forth. Practicing for a year makes us healthy and frees us from death. One can even see into the future and be able to hear words spoken far away. Venom cannot stay in the body even if one has a serious illness. When the mind is settled, one is liberated from all poisons, whether fixed or moving, even if the skin is cut open. Between the two is found Rajada, the central place, the bindu itself.

Amrita regenerates us. It produces youth and destroys old age. The wise man, having produced a drink of fresh amrita in this place, is freed from wrinkles and white hair. He is freed of all illness. For him, no death exists. Through his yoga, he remains always above death. One should worship the rasa located at the root of the palate. It destroys illness. Standing or walking, sleeping or awake, eating or engaging in sexual relations, one must always generate the rasa that condenses inside one's mouth. After having centered one's mind in the heart, finding oneself in a state of inner silence, one avoids death for many years, because one has the choice of dying when the time seems right. When death approaches, one can destroy it in a half ghantika. Devi, the revelation has been given to you completely. Hide well the illusion of time."

✤ Patala Seven ✤

Devi says: "O Natha, You who are my refuge, speak to me of the three tattvas and of the knowledge relating to old age and decline, to the destroyer of fever and death."

Bhairava says: "Mother of Heroes! Listen to what relates to the knowledge of old age, graying hair, and decline. On the first day of the lunar fortnight, one should meditate on residing in the Devi's chakra. Sweet-faced One! We are going to visualize the top of the head in a white color, like the Moon, as if a lake of the purest ghee is nourishing the chakra of the bones. One must meditate on the top of the cranium where there's a black mark from which an ointment is flowing, destroying wrinkles and gray hair. From now on, O Devi! Listen carefully to the second method. At the spot where, from the point of view of yoga, there is located the stem of the Adhara chakras, which is cool, fresh, and dissolves in the Brahmarandhra, one must visualize the flow of the black ointment. One must know that, by nature, the Sun is hostile and the Moon is friendly. By meditating on a single black spot as well as by wearing black clothing, one can be freed of all the setbacks and confusions generated by life, and freed of all the ills. He who masters the control of the senses and who, adorned with a variety of flowers, lives in a beautiful desert location, offers boiled rice and perfumed incense for a period of six months—such a one obtains the powers of the siddha yoginis. He is then their equal, like the god of love worshiped by deva kanyas. Varanane! One should visualize the three centers placed in the Brahmagranthi, each one being dissolved in this bit of Brahma that resembles a fragment of collyrium.

Dear One! By using this substance, one should gratify all

the pores of the skin and all the areas of the body. By meditating this way for six months, one is completely nourished and becomes healthy and young—about that there can be no doubt. One should visualize the sixteen petals inside the pinda, each one having a part of the substance of black color and adorned with the sixteen vowels. In dissolving this sphere in the Brahmarandhra with devotion during an arduous practice of six months, one is perfectly nourished and one becomes youthful. About this there is no doubt. One becomes like Kamadeva, the God of Love, by being unified at the place where the yoginis live, and by meditating on them and on oneself as being black in color. Let us meditate on the image of an eight-petalled chakra, colored white like the Moon, and located where the spine meets the skull, that is, where one's hairline begins. We can gratify our bodies thanks to this light. At the end of six months or a year, we will be perfectly satiated, liberated from fever and death, without the slightest pain or physical illness. We will then be the equal of the hosts of yoginis, the cause of both creation and dissolution. By making use of this substance, visualizing it penetrating each hair and the pores of the skin, one becomes very fortunate like the God of Love. One's head of hair stays abundant and black. In the first place, one finds liberation from pain. In the second place, from illness. Third, one becomes eloquent like jewels that fascinate us; fourth, one speaks gently of love; fifth, one is then able to hear everything that is said at a distance; sixth, one is able to leave the ground; seventh, one enters into union with the yoginis, and eighth, one is liberated from fever and illnesses. Ninth, one can travel at high speed; tenth, one can take on various appearances. The eleventh result is that one attains peace and that one liberates oneself in three possible ways. The twelfth result is that one is worshipped like the god Shiva. One can go wherever one wants through the simple power of will. Only a Kaulika can accomplish such feats. If one does not know the Kaula shastras, the Kaula gurus, the Kaula mantras, and the Kaula Shiva, unless one is a Natha of the Kaula Agama, one is only a simple pashu. Someone dishonest who has the pretension of being a Natha is deceiving himself. He who is a victim of his own ignorance will certainly be destroyed. He will be left to wander confused, paralyzed, ill, and struck down. However, a Kaula who devotes himself to this practice for seven nights is purified thanks to all the rays of the supreme bindu that he has seen and touched. Knowledge concerning the cessation of decrepitude has been explained to you, O You Who Are Worshipped by Yoginis. By uniting with Kamakala, one can put an end to old age. Thus we have explained to you the secret and the characteristics of the being who has changed inwardly."

❧ Patala Eight ❧

Devi says: "It is very difficult to understand because it is really occult knowledge that harbors the greatest of all secrets. Bhairava! How is Kula created from Akula? What are the natures of the Ksetraja, born from the womb, the Pithaja, born of a sacred place, the Yogaja, born of yoga, the Mantraja born of mantras, sahaja, born of the spontaneous, and Kulaja, born of Kula and the sixty-four yoginis? O My Lord! Speak to me of the Kula siddha, of the nature and the implementation of the sadhana. Explain all the rules concerning the guru sadhana."

Bhairava says: "Listen to this specific point, O Mother of Yoginis and Heroines! In a desolate spot, adorned with fragrant and perfumed flower garlands, one will offer fish and meat that is to be consumed and one will enjoy drinking wine to attain a state of ecstasy. When one is united with Shakti, she will be Sahaja, Kulaja, or Antyaja. At present, I'm going to speak to you about individual characteristics. When Sadhana is conducted in the company of one's spouse, she is Sahaja. We affirm this. A veshya woman is Kulaja and an untouchable woman is Antyaja. The external aspects have been revealed. Devi, listen attentively now to their internal forms. When one meditates on the fact that the body of Devi exults in an ecstatic love, that it is ready for sexual union, she becomes Sahaja Shakti. The Kulaja is a pile of letters, the essence of Kula. What can then be unknown to her? The internal aspects are of three kinds and the external forms are of three kinds also.

My Dear One! Now I am going to speak about the Antyaja. Listen, O Devi, to how she is placed. She is the Khageshvari; from the purest of limpid crystals. She wears a necklace of pearls with a white mark on her forehead, the radiant Mahashakti. The

great Shaktis are themselves the Antyaja that constitutes the Devi
Vyoma Malini, whose mouth is full of betel, her hair disheveled,
adorned with sandalwood paste, and soaked in musk displaying
an attitude of joy and fullness. The yoginis and the viras must do
sadhana using two vessels, each doing so separately.

We should do the sadhana of the sixty-four or fifty-five
yoginis.

Depending on the kind of Shakti, we pay homage to the circle
of yoginis and viras by all wearing red clothing, that is like wearing
a beautiful bracelet or a necklace of limpid gems. By following this
path, while making use of Kulacara, individuals can enter fully
into the Kula. We must worship Mahadevi as the Ksetrajas situated in various locations, places like Karavira, Mahakala, Devikoti,
Varanasi, Prayag, Caritra, Ekamra, Attahasa, and Jayanti. This is
where these Ksetrajas reside. My Dear One! The Ksetrajas origi-
nate from the heart of these main locations.

> *Hrim shrim hrim shrim* to the feet of the
>   Konkananaja
> *Hrim* three times to the feet of the Kalambaju
> *Hrim* three times to the feet of the Mangalaja
> *Hrim* three times to the feet of the Siddhaja
> *Hrim* three times to the feet of the Vacchaja
> *Hrim* three times to the feet of the Shivaja
> *Hrim* three times to the feet of the Shri Icchaja
> *Hrim* three times to the feet of the Aryaja
> *Hrim* three times to the feet of the Viraja
> *Hrim* three times to the feet of the
>   Tribhubanaja
> *Hrim* three times to the feet of the
>   Varaharupaja

Hrim three times to the feet of the Krita
Yugaja

Devi, here are the places venerated by the siddhas in the course of four yugas. First of all, one recites the formulation *'Hrim shrim,'* and after that one says their name. The Ksetrajas have been declared. Now I will speak to you about the Pithajas.

The first pitha that arose is called Kamakhya. There are seven lesser pithas of Devi. They are places where siddhas dwell. The second pitha is known as Purnagiri. Oddiyana is a Mahapitha, and several lesser pithas are associated with it. Arvudama is a pitha having lesser pithas. There are pithas, upapithas, sandohas, ksetras and upaksetras. My Dear One! Listen now to the puja rules of the pitha divinities.

Hrim three times to the feet of Mahalaksmaja
Hrim three times to the feet of Kusumanangaja
Hrim three times to the feet of Shuklaja
Hrim three times to the feet of Pralambaja
Hrim three times to the feet of Pulindaja
Hrim three times to the feet of Shabaraja
Hrim three times to the feet of Krsnaja
Hrim three times to the feet of Lacchaja
Hrim three times to the feet of Nandaja
Hrim three times to the feet of Bhadraja
Hrim three times to the feet of Kalambaja
Hrim three times to the feet of Campaja
Hrim three times to the feet of Dhavalaja
Hrim three times to the feet of Hidimbaja
Hrim three times to the feet of Mahamayaja

The yoginis who bestow their favors all come from pithas, upapithas, and sandohas! Worshipping these, the Mothers can accomplish everything. The siddha who successfully practices yoga and recites mantras gives birth to Yogaja Mothers and Mantraja Mothers. These Mothers arise from his mantras.

The Sahaja Mothers of Devi are very powerful and very terrifying. They are beautiful and red in color. They allow even a pashu to attain a celestial state. These Mothers give birth to living beings. They are behind the genesis of the being in the womb.

They are called Brahmi, Maheshvari, Kaumari, Vaisnavi, Varahi, Vajrahasta, Yogeshvari, and Aghoreshi. It has to do with the famous Matrka, which emanates from Devi, it is said. Besides, there are other Doorway Protectresses that were at the origin of the existence of the Cosmos. In small communities, in towns, in hamlets, always and everywhere, one must worship them as well as their guru siddhas. Planets, nagas, devas, yoginis, siddhas, all beings worship the eight Kulas. Now I will declare the eight categories and their eight modifications.

> *Hrim A Hrim Hrim Im Hrim Hrim Um Hrim*
> *Hrim Rm Hrim Hrim Aim Hrim Hrim Om*
> *Hrim Hrim Hrim Ah Hrim*

This is the first, Devi.
Listen now to the eight vidyas:

> *Hrim Ksa Hrim Lah Hrim Hah Hrim Sa Hrim*
> *Sa Hrim Sha Hrim Va Hrim Va Hrim Ra.*

Hrim Klrim is Kaulika, Bhairavi. One must combine the vidya in eight ways. The first of the eight we have already spoken about.

Just as that was formed by a combination, all the yoginis must be considered as being able to combine in this way. Multiplying eight by eight gives the sixty-four yoginis. This is consistent with the order assigned to them.

The first chakra confers the power to unite with the yoginis, the power to make oneself small, and among the eight siddhis, effective attainment in meditation and sadhana. About this there can be no doubt.

With the puja and the dhyana (meditation) centered on the second chakra, one acquires the power to hypnotize all beings, the ability to break or throw objects at a distance, and the ability to subjugate others. Whoever practices frequently the method of the third great chakra can subtly slip into someone else's body and, in addition, he is able to access visions of the future.

The fourth chakra is a marvelous provider of the powers of calming, liberation, and sensual pleasuring. If one venerates this chakra using a person's image during meditation, one is capable of instantly paralyzing someone with a single gesture. In addition, one gains the power of invisibility and of hearing conversations whether they are close by or distant. Whoever speaks a part of the shastra mantra gains the power to catch in a net with the mantra, it is said. He can become one with all beings using his own power. In six months, he becomes a perfected being, O Beloved of the Yoginis! He is liberated from the power of time and he becomes a second Kamadeva.

By meditating and carrying out sadhana on the fifth chakra, one is capable of speaking like a rishi, moving like the wind, and halting someone's conversation.

The sixth chakra bestows dharma (teaching), artha (power), and moksha (liberation). Whoever practices meditation and attains his sadhana on the seventh chakra for long periods will obtain the power to enslave others. He will display the ability to paralyze, subjugate others, and he will liberate himself from the chains of samsara.

The eighth chakra is the vehicle that sets Iccha Siddhi in motion. It allows one to cause death and to travel far away, and in addition it bestows the power to generate paralysis or illusion in others. He who is established in this great chakra is beloved by the Kulas, by the yoginis. It is only by being aware of the sixty-four rules that the siddhis are granted; otherwise they are not granted. The secret order of the sixty-four yoginis has thus been stated by me, and I have done so in the clearest of terms. You must remember this with devotion."

✢ Patala Nine ✢

Bhairava says: "O Beauteous One to See! Henceforth, I will speak to you about the gurus and the siddhas. I will describe to you the lineage of the yoginis, all the siddhas and yoginis, the Khecaris who traverse the skies, all Mothers, all the Bhucaris who move about on the Earth, the Gocari yoginis that our senses perceive, all those belonging to Ksetra, the sacred places, and those produced by the mantras, yoga, and the pithas. I will speak about Sahaja, Kulaja, and all the Doorway Protectoresses, as well as those who are born from the womb during the Krita, Dvapara, Treta, and Kali Yugas, the various ages of the world. I will speak about the siddhi yoginis worshipped during the four yugas. Of all the secrets, this is the highest and the most powerful. It is revealed to you from love."

Devi says: "My body, consumed by the fever of love, is now refreshed. O Kaulesha! By Your Grace I have been instructed about the elements of real knowledge. Now I would like to hear you speak about the sadhana of the Siddha Gurus."

Bhairava says: "Devi, True Self of Kula! Please listen now to the rules concerning the siddha gurus whom we must worship:

Shri Vishva Pada, Shri Vicitra Pada,
Shri Shveta Pada, Shri Bhatta Pada,
Shri Macchendra Pada, Shri Brihis Pada,
Shri Vindhya Pada, Shri Shabara Pada,
Shri Mahendra Pada, Shri Candra Pada,
Shri Hidini Pada, Shri Samudra Pada,
Shri Lavana Pada, Shri Dumbara Pada,
Shri Deva Pada, Shri Dhivara Pada,
Shri Simhala Pada, Shri Ogini Pada,

Guru, Guru's Guru, highest Guru. One
must worship the Lakinis, the Dakinis, the
Sakinis, the Kakinis, and the Yakinis.

After having recited *Hrim* at the beginning, one should recite *Hrim* at the end. One must place these two syllables before each of the names. It is impossible to speak of a subject any higher than this knowledge of perfection arising from the yoginis in the course of the Siddha Kulagama. In the terrible, horror-filled hell (Raurava) of the Kali Yuga were born sixteen siddhas who became Kaula initiates. O Viravandita! I speak of the names of the siddhas of the Krita Yuga, the Dvapara Yuga, and the Treta Yuga. Listen, O Beauteous One to See!

Mrsni Pada, Avatara Pada, Surya Pada, Dyuti
Pada, Om Pada, Vyaghra Pada, Harini Pada,
Panca Shikhi Pada, Komala Pada,
Lambodara Pada.

These Maha Siddhas whom we have just mentioned are the Kula Kaula Avataras, Devesi. In the course of the four Yugas, each one of them independently set forth the Kula path. In meditating on them, various processes are accomplished. The terrible origin of this path of the Kaulas is of unlimited extent! It is the heart of the quintessence of the Maha Kaula, O My Beautiful One! Called Iccha Yogini by the siddhas with their supreme free wills, it was then revealed by Iccha to the Khecari; then it was newly expressed by the Khecari to the Little Mothers. The Mothers revealed it to the Bhucari, O Kuleshvari. Subsequently, the Kauliki Yoginis communicated the understanding of it to an initiate in the Kula Way. Even if our faults arise from having reincarnated 400,000 times, one gains merit in the Kaulacara and, in receiving this knowledge, one becomes a free and fulfilled Maha Siddha, Beloved of the Yoginis."

❦ Patala Ten ❦

Devi says: "Just now, O Natha, Lord of the Suras! speak to me of the full effect of the pinda, the Self contained and situated in Fire. Bhairava, if you take pleasure in my company, speak to me of this Fire. The elements of knowledge have already been revealed to me. O Kaulesha, once again I ask you! Speak O Lord! O Natha, I have doubts about the sixty-four locations of infinite extent. Explain to me the characteristics of each of the chakras, each one separately. Lord Bhairava, reveal to me the secret placement of the chakras, and what is the complete result of meditation on these centers."

Bhairava says: "Very Dear Mahadevi, this is a difficult question even for the gods. Sweet-faced One, I will speak frankly of that out of love for you.

Lam Lim Lüm Lrm Lum Laim Laum Lah
Ham Him Hum Hrm Hum Haim Haum Hah
Sam Sim Sum Srm Sum Saim Saum Sah
Sham Shim Shun Shrem Shum Shaim Shaum Shah
Vam Vim Vüm Vrm Vum Vaim Vaum Vah
Hlam Hlim Hlum Hlrm Hlum Hlaim Hlaum Hlah.

The letter *'Ksa'* is located in the Brahmarandhra, *'La'* in the forehead, *'Ha'* between the eyes, *'Sa'* in the mouth, *'Sa'* in the throat, *'Sha'* in the heart, *'Va'* in the navel, and *'Hla'* in the genitals.

My Dear One! Learn the meditation on the placement of these chakras.

The first of the eight chakras is a celestial eight-petalled lotus, like a pure limpid crystal, a divine flame or fire, lacking any imperfection. It is free of all duality, free of the flames of cruelty, and even stripped of the void. We must avoid the slightest disruption, and put sama consciousness into practice. From then on, we are able to make out the future, having united with the unshakable circle of time. We can know what is spoken great distances away, we can confer favors and paralyze others, we can seize and subjugate pashus, or destroy them or kill them, we can be immortal, always truthful and balanced, eloquent like the siddhas, and able to fulfill our desires.

We must meditate on the second eight-petalled chakra, which is also as brilliant as a beautiful pure flame. In this way, we can vanquish death and be at the start of great tumult. By meditating calmly on this complex form, one becomes an emperor among kings, one who can accomplish everything one wants. Always engaged in the path of love, being similar to Kruddha—such a one can destroy everything in the three worlds, living beings as well as inanimate objects.

The third chakra is the one that gives birth to nine tattvas. After having meditated for six months on the guru, who is situated in this adhara, we can accomplish whatever we desire: the effects of old age are destroyed, one is able to see far into the distance and immobilize others even from a distance of one hundred yojanas. In a solitary spot we must meditate on this complex form.

The fourth chakra is the source of peace. It increases happiness and contentment. In always meditating on it, we become immortal, eloquent, and victorious over death and illness. The daily practice of it sends death flying. An ongoing practice on this great chakra, during a period of sixteen seasons, makes it possible to generate destruction in one day and one night. O Surasundari!

The fifth great lotus has eight petals. We must always meditate on it as being the color of smoke, and then it becomes possible to shake the foundations of the Three Worlds. It generates eloquence and avoids untimely death. It allows one to both enslave and to paralyze.

If we meditate with devotion on the sixth royal chakra, which is all ablaze and has a pericarp of eight petals that is as luminous as molten gold and is (considered to be) the source of Iccha Siddhi, we can see the future, obtain the anima and seven other siddhis. About that there is no doubt, Dear Mahadevi!

The seventh chakra is as luminous as the Full Moon and is propitious. Inside the body, it confers both happiness and liberation. It destroys fever and death, and it allows you to penetrate the bodies of others. What cannot be accomplished? One becomes the best within a group of individuals.

Beautiful to contemplate! The eighth chakra is embellished with eight petals. It confers dharma, artha, kama, and moksha.

When we meditate on the chakras as being red, they always confer authority over others. If yellow, they cause paralysis. If pure crystal, they confer liberation and, if black, then death. If the color of smoke, they give the power to uproot. In meditating on them being a white that is as pure as cow's milk, one obtains Mrtyuinjaya. One can cause great tumult, paralysis; cause the intellectual and physical abilities of others to be lost; and many other things.

One should always meditate on the eight chakras with the help of a beautiful, intense, and luminous flame that one moves eight times, one by one, through each of the centers. Through one's own willpower, one becomes the Lord of Breath capable of generating enthusiasm by being united with Kanchuki Devi herself."

Devi says: "Now Bhairava! I would like to know about creation in the Mahakaulas."

⁂ Patala Eleven ⁂

Devi says: "Mahadeva! Speak to me from the depth of your being about the characteristics of nonduality as well as of food. Freed from all these doubts, one may certainly attain liberation."

Bhairava says: "What you are requesting, Devi, I will explain completely, thus freeing you from doubt. He who always establishes himself in nonduality knows success. He who takes action in the dualist way is subject to the influence of yogis. Devi, he who fails in this simple method is just a pashu, no doubt about that. One should disregard dualist thought and take inspiration from the path of unity.

Now I'm going to reveal to you the five nectars. Of all secrets, this is the greatest one. This should be known to the couple trained by the Kula adepts, the Kula children, the sadhakas, the very ones who seek the kamasiddhi and those who dwell in Kula land. O Exquisite One to Admire! This was formerly accomplished by the Kula siddhas. If one becomes aware of this, one becomes a spiritually perfected being, O One Beloved by the Yoginis! One can succeed in whatever one undertakes by using the five nectars. Then one can gather the effects of the siddhis and become like the host of yoginis. O Devi! They appear charming to all those who worship them with an oblation of the five nectars. After having conducted the rites with this offering, one becomes immediately equal to the yoginis. He who is shown how to act and knows yoga should act in such a way. He will become a realized being, of that there is no doubt. He will be liberated of all obstacles and freed from attachments like the host of yoginis. His thoughts will be clear and simple. In the Kaula Agama the five eternal and pure substances are ashes, woman's nectar, sperm, blood, and clarified butter all mixed together.

Devi! During the two daily rites, one should carefully offer all of those in order to fulfill one's desires, offering also beef, cow's milk, curds, and ghee. During rites to fulfill one's desires and during acts of kamasiddhi, the great recompense is what one must do in the Kaula Agama. This is very true and without any doubt. In all that is done following other paths I give neither siddhi nor liberation. Listen carefully to the list of other offerings. One must offer and one must eat dogs, cats, camels, jackals, horses, sea tortoises, turtles, bears, crabs, porcupines, cuckoos, and various other Kula substances: wild boar, deer, buffalo, elephant, and other dishes such as fish. It is important to show discrimination in this affair; otherwise one would become a pashu in seven successive births. One must worship the host of yoginis and offer appropriate things to eat. My Dear One! From now on, one can eat whatever one wants. One should have wine and eat as much as one wants in order to have a long life. Three kinds of cakes should be offered, as well as various kinds of fruit and lemons. According to the rule, it is necessary to offer wine made from the fruit of trees, roots, or flowers as an oblation to the devatas. In the course of rites for specific desires, it is necessary to offer meat, wine, and sweetened alcohol. One must observe nonduality here and never do otherwise. Anyone who takes another path instead of the nondual path commits a sin. Such a one will fall into a terrible hell, ending up in the Raurava Hell. Should a pashu act in the nondual way as I have explained, then he will be surrounded by yoginis and will be renowned in Kula. It's a great secret and one that should be hidden, just as a son remains hidden in the uterus of his mother. One should carefully conceal the nondual way. Doing so, one becomes like Kamadeva—powerful, fecund, possessing anima and other siddhis. The guru is himself, the siddha is himself, the student is himself, Shiva is himself. Those fettered by ignorance do not know this, whereas those who know are already liberated. One should perceive perfumes and foul-smelling odors as having the same nature. Sureshvari, just as a petal of the lotus in water is without stain, a yogi knows neither merit nor sin. A person in whom this mental tendency has flourished makes no distinction between murdering a Brahmin and the Vedic sacrifice of Ashvamedha. He makes no distinction between bathing in sacred springs and entering into contact with barbarians. He remains at the heart of the void, in balance (*sama*), having no contact with anything around him, and he is fully satisfied. One should never devote oneself to dualistic yoga. One must not offer oblation while afflicted by lust, cruelty, envy, greed, or idleness. Instead, a simple nondual approach is needed.

One should always consume blood and sperm. My Very Dear One! This is the oblation of the siddhas and the yoginis. One must offer flesh to the shakinis (and to the other terrible divinities). My Very Dear One! Listen now to what is offered to the devis. One must offer buk flowers, ashes, blood, sperm, wine, wood of the Brahma tree, and so forth, flowers of all sorts, perfume, incense, betel, music, and red clothing. The siddhas and the devatas are pleased with the red color used during acts of worship; these acts should be offered in full awareness. Anyone who is satisfied offering only vegetarian food incurs three additional incarnations. Greediness and wavering always bring disgrace on the Kula shastra. One is praised by the siddhas for seeing and touching Shakti's blood, as well as for the sexual pleasure from knowing the Kula Way for six months.

My Very Dear One! A Brahmin goes to heaven thanks to endless ablutions of his feet and his mouth, whereas he who often makes a tilaka of kunda, a gola or an udbhava of blood can destroy various illnesses such as leprosy and smallpox. He is freed of all sickness in the same way a serpent sheds his skin when molting. Such a being is as brilliant as the sun at its zenith and is beloved by the yoginis. He is equal to the Absolute, the Conqueror of Three Worlds, who performs oblation only by following the way of non-duality. Devi, one must accomplish all that resides in Iccha Shakti and not offer oblation unless it be in accord with Will. Oblation according to the nondual way has thus been declared in the *Jnana Nirnaya Tantra*."

❧ Patala Twelve ❧

Devi says: "I am enveloped by joy. My mind is satisfied and thrilled with happiness! O Bhairava, I would like to question you further. Now I wish to know the nature of the simple path of acting as a Kaula and the nature of the vessels."

Bhairava says: "O Viracamunda, listen to the characteristics of the vessels and how to act. One can be like a child, a madman, or a king. One can pass out, or have an independent state of mind. One can be a Hero and a Lord, be like a gandharva, or someone naked. One can be a Tridandin, or someone who sells knowledge.

O Resplendent One! The way is to act according to one's own will, while being aware of both the Akula and Devi's Kula. One should always worship Bhairava with the Kulas and the Siddhas. One should always worship, three times, one's own guru. He is the cause of one's own being. He who wants to obtain both happiness and liberation should make a gift to his guru of his personal belongings, his speech, his mind, and his actions. On the way of nonduality of the Kaula Agama, devotion to the guru constitutes the primordial act. Whatever one wants can be obtained by means of the way of nonduality."

Devi says: "Deva! By your grace, you have revealed to me the characteristics of conduct. Once again, I ask you: What is the best of all the vessels?"

Bhairava says: "Devi! Listen attentively to the nature of the vessels. A Kaulika's vessel can be made of clay, tortoise shell, bell metal, copper, iron, gold, silver, pearl, conch shell, glass, horn, wood, or stone. Of all of these the best would be Vishvamitra's skull. After having crafted this object, if one drinks, enjoys, and eats from it, one becomes a Lord. One is even above a Lord and even greater than that. One must drink wine exclusively from this large vessel in the shape of a coconut. Devi, the various vessels and how to use them have been explained. What else do you want to know?"

Devi says: "Lord of the Word! You have engendered a divine state in me. Lord God! Through your grace, I have come to know the characteristics of knowledge."

✤ Patala Thirteen ✤

Bhairava says: "Lady of Heroes! Listen to the knowledge that bestows liberation. In knowing this, a jiva enjoys liberation both above and below. In the animate and inanimate worlds, one should always recite '*Hamsa Hamsa.*' Having heard this, one becomes fortunate like a Lord of Heaven who has gained the opportunity of spiritual liberation. The Three Worlds and the Cosmos emanate from this great wonder, which remains stable in eternity. After becoming aware of this great secret, one knows everything. By this means only, beings are liberated. All actions would be futile without it. In being distanced from that, one will never know what is auspicious or inauspicious. Without this, neither mind nor citta exist. Taste or meditation will not be able to exist. Those who know this are freed from mind and non-mind. When we perceive the phenomenon, that is, the letters of Hamsa, in the thousand-petalled lotus, it appears like a garland of joyous blossoms. Anyone who becomes like this is freed from merit and demerit. He progresses on the grand path of divinity and enjoys full awareness. There is no doubt about this. This is the essence of liberation, the bindu in the center of the lotus petals, no doubt about it. '*I*' resides in the anus, '*I ksu*' in the genitals, '*I yau*' in the navel, '*I mau*' in the mouth, '*I vau*' in the right nostril, '*I lau*' in the left cavity, '*I rau*' in the right cavity, '*I do*' in the right ear, '*I shau*' in the left ear, '*I hrau*' on the eyebrows, '*Sam tam*' on the forehead, '*Sam am*' in the left ear. '*Sah yam*' in the right ear, '*Sa pam*' on the left eye, '*Sa ri*' on the right eye, '*Vah tam*' on the left nostril, '*Sah pum*' on the right nostril, '*Sah rum*' in the mouth, '*Sah yam*' in the navel, '*Sah sum*' in the lingam or the yoni, and '*Sah lam*' inside the anus. Devi, he who knows this cycle concerning the placement of the centers knows liberation, there is no doubt. He has attained the supreme consciousness that I have spoken to you about. Devi, when one meditates thus in one's skull, one becomes Lord of the Body."

⚜ Patala Fourteen ⚜

Devi says: "I have doubts about how one frees oneself from time, how to be instantaneously freed of the chakras, and I have doubts about the nature of the siddhis, about the center of the body, and about how to leave one's body."

Bhairava says: "Devi, listen to the marvelous path that is the bestower of greatness. My Very Dear One! The path of supreme Kaula is not known to Brahma, Vishnu, and the gods; it is not known to the dimwitted, the gandharvas, the kinnaras, the yakshas, the asuras, or the ascetics. One should never give the Kaulika essence to slow pupils, to those lacking in devotion to Kula or the guru, to the deceitful, to confused-minded disciples, to the foolish, or to those who are weak or liars. One should never make a gift of it to the enemies of saints, gods, or fire. He who initiates such persons as disciples will be destroyed in his body. One should make a gift of it only to those who have been tested, those who know that the guru is the fount of knowledge, those who are humble and pious, those who are free of all cruelty, those who are stable, those who are freed from desire, those who are discreet, those who one is sure about, those who are dressed properly, those who are pleasant, those who are gifted with intelligence, those who are always pious toward the gods, fire, and saints, and the yoginis. He who engenders this kind of devotion in his disciple when initiating him will enjoy a long life. One should never give knowledge of the Kaulikas to someone disloyal, a materialist, a breaker of vows, the enemy of the yoginis, an abuser of the guru's knowledge, the lustful, the cruel, the blameworthy, or those who revile Shiva and the Kula Bhairava.

Bhavini Devi! Listen now to the presentation concerning the

chakras that you asked me about earlier. When one concentrates on the first chakra, the root chakra, this bestows an increase in immense good fortune and an increase in the field of consciousness. First of all, one experiences a shivering, which is followed by a trembling of the hands, feet, and head. Moreover, difficulty speaking appears, and so on. The person becomes entirely immersed in mantras and mudras and is able to leave the body, to speak poetically, and is able to see the future. Devi! Such a person becomes free of the illusion of time, and his body is endlessly regenerated. Sundari! By destroying all traces of old age such as graying hair and wrinkles, it is certain one becomes like Khecara. O Varanane! By blending into the Kaula root chakra, one receives the eight siddhis.

Listen, Devi, to the marvelous characteristics of another adhara. Four finger widths above the root center is located the Devi chakra. Parvati purified herself by putting this discipline into practice. One experiences a trembling and difficulty speaking; then one is immersed in mudras. One becomes aware of shastras never previously heard, as well as numerous mantras and mudras. One becomes like Khecara, able to both subdue and attract others, while also being freed of fever and the illusion of death and time. That way one obtains the patala siddhis by becoming Khecara and having a long life. Thus, the characteristics of the adhara have been explained to you.

Now I'm going to speak to you about the characteristics of the Brahma granthi. A quick meditation on this center is rich and fertile. One experiences various effects such as the sensation of vibrations and difficulties speaking. One becomes clairaudient, capable of making cities totter, and one can even foretell the future. Devi! One is freed from the illusion of time by becoming immortal, and by acquiring the power of poetic expression.

In conquering anima and the other siddhis, one attains the state of Kamadeva. Devi! There you have the characteristics of Brahma granthi. O Beauteous Kalyani! Listen now to what resides at a higher level. Above one's head of hair there revolves a center that is like a flaming light bursting forth and radiating from itself. He who meditates in secret on this center for seven nights will experience trembling and vibration; he will become eloquent and show signs of fainting. He becomes able to enter into the bodies of others, subjugating and attracting others to himself. He becomes able to see at a distance, to make wrinkles and his gray hair disappear. His body regenerates itself. Through continual practice, he will become equal to khecari and will be instructed in love. Thus, I have told you about the Kaulika center above one's head of hair. Suvrata, the nature of Vrsanottha Kula has been declared to you.

Mother of Heroes who grants favors to the Heroes, listen now attentively! I will speak of the very ones who devote themselves to the Vahni Kaula. If one centers oneself steadily in awareness for half a moment, one immediately becomes established in that awareness. One is capable of halting another's speaking, and so forth. With a single gesture, one can leave one's body, subjugate and attract others, destroy fever and death, enter into the bodies of others and subjugate them. One is able to shake the world. Certainly, a person skilled in this Kaulika path will obtain the powers of Uttistha, of Khadga, and of Patala. Through arduous practice, anyone can assume the appearance that she wants.

Once again, I will declare another method—that of the ultimate Kaula sadbhava. After having meditated on the center of one's heart, one is then settled there. From then on, one can obtain samadhi, paralyze and subjugate others, and so forth. All that, while experiencing a sensation of vibration in the hands, the head, the feet—in fact, in the whole body. You Who Grant Your

Favors! Know that one becomes good at describing objects and making cities quake. O Sulocana! Based on constant inner practice, one may sexually excite the gandharvis, the celestial musicians, the kinnaris, the demigods, the yakshis, the magic beings, the inhabitants of the abysses, the asuris, the demons, and the vidyadharis, those who hold worldly knowledge. There is no doubt about this. One obtains the highest state. One becomes clairaudient and able to enter cities and subjugate their inhabitants. One destroys death. One unites with yoginis; one becomes one with them and benefits from a long life. The revelation concerning the Kulasadbhava, which is stationed in the heart, is complete. Now I will speak to you about another school. O Makaradhvaje! Listen to me. After having established one's consciousness in the well of the throat center, one can proclaim and describe the true essence of the shastras, thanks to one's own Shakti. One may see beyond the future, as well as the infinite circle of time and space, becoming free from death, strong, immortal, and radiant, liberated from fever and other illnesses, liberated from physical degeneration. Like Kruddha, one gains the ability to shake the Three Worlds and all that is found there, animate beings or inanimate objects. He who puts this method into practice will not only be the equal of Brahma, Vishnu, and Rudra, but of all three at the same time. This Kaula path of Pada Uttistha is knowledge concerning the non-Self. This privileged knowing allows one to become like the god of love, independent and fully realized. O Kaula Devi, the true doctrine of knowledge is thus declared. It is stationed in the throat. One should apply it ceaselessly in order to obtain the desired results.

At present, the secret of Urdhveshvara destroys all illness. After forming the rasa above the head, one should sprinkle it all over one's whole body. My Very Dear One, he who assiduously puts this exercise into practice is able to destroy objects in a muhurta. In an instant, one is freed from illness, affliction, death, and fever. Illnesses are destroyed just as a stag is killed by the lion. In an instant, a disease like leprosy is wiped out. Mahadevi! By using beautiful sweating, one can halt aging. A person becomes immortal by engaging in "sweating milk." Devi! A person becomes independent by using ghee to stimulate sweating. One should constrain consciousness to remain in a chakra by concentrating the breathing on the nose chakra. In this way, one can obtain the siddhi of eloquence in becoming like Kamadeva, by attracting divine maidens, the devis, the yakshis, and the vidyadharis. Thanks to offerings of sweet meats, lights, wicks dipped in oil, sweets, saffron, and other food, one can attract many celestial maidens and have them love you. Through the flow of celestial semen, one can attain anima, laghiman, and the eight other siddhis. My Very Dear One! Only by using celestial semen can one become a yogi. He who does otherwise cannot be a real yogi. You Whose Words Are So Sweet! This divine secret concerning the chakra is impossible to attain by assiduous practice. It is only granted by grace. It is the real yoga. Greater than this secret is another secret, that of the great yogini Kaula. Through continual practice, it is the source of the essence of the greatest mysticism. Making use of this method, one obtains anima and the other siddhis, becoming able to see events happening at a great distance. This occurs through applying oneself continuously, there is no doubt about it. One can resuscitate the dead, move into the incarnated bodies of others, create images that speak, break pots and stone. It is possible to seize and subjugate pashus and to regenerate one's own body. One becomes like Brahma, Vishnu, Yama, Indra, Varuna, and Vayu. O Varanane! One rules in one's body like the Moon in the heavens. The gandharvas, the kinnaras, the yakshas, the nagas, the vidyadharas, the ten million celestial chariots (stars), the planets, the macrocosm, all movement, the Three Worlds with their inhabitants, animate beings and inanimate objects— all these are perceived as having their abode in the human body. Through constant and assiduous meditation, one can perceive this inside oneself. O Devi! Our being becomes like Shiva, able to create and to destroy ten thousand million things. An assiduous practice bestows the eight kinds of siddhis of which the shastras speak. O Varanane! One should grant this Kaula knowledge only to beings who deserve it and no one else! Being adored by all, one obtains the siddhis and one becomes my equal. In the Guru Kaula Agama, one should always intensively practice devotion toward the devi using sexual worship. Without a doubt, one must always carefully hide this revelation.

Now I will speak to you about something even bigger. Listen, Kula Bhavini! Focus your attention on the forehead center with the collection of Sanskrit letters. Then one becomes eloquent while experiencing trembling in all the limbs. Then Nada comes out and one perceives a strong breeze. By continuing to apply one-self in this way, one can assume any appearance one wants.

Greater still is the supreme secret. Listen to me attentively. Meditate on the center between the eyebrows, the place where the group of letters reside. By practicing assiduously this mode of wor-ship, one can become an eternal hero capable of rejecting ordinary rules. O You Who Are Loved by the Yoginis! One becomes the principle of creation and dissolution by being freed from fever and death forever. There is no doubt about this. By applying this method revealed through knowledge, one becomes a liberated being.

Now I will speak to you about the characteristics of having knowledge and skill concerning the cracks of the skull. In prac-ticing this method ceaselessly, one accesses knowledge, freeing oneself from illness and death. Having become my equal, one becomes the origin of dissolution and creation. One plays in the full state of independence, having become one with Iccha. Moving ahead on the Kaulika path, one always finds one's full balance and liberation. Listen now to the ability that allows the mind to see at a distance. This is achieved thanks to a secret center located inside the skull on which one applies one's attention; from then on, the ability to leave one's body at will appears. One no longer has to fear injury caused by insects, tigers, lions, or elephants. My Very Dear One! We must meditate often on forms following Kula knowledge that belongs to the authentic lineage of the gurus. This essence bestows liberation. Consequently, with each one of our efforts, we must become aware of the Kula characteristics. Then calm is installed like a full vessel, and one is as stable as a strong wall. In becoming established in the practice of these methods, one becomes equal to the yoginis.

Now I am going to speak about something even more grand. Listen, O Beloved of the Viras! Let us meditate on ourselves as being not water, not fire, not earth, not air, not ether; as not being above or below or in the middle; as something that is not mineral, not vegetable, or animal. This is done by situating oneself in the unmani state of mind. After meditating on himself as being empty and not empty, freed of all thought, without any movement, the wise man becomes as big as a village. Balanced by this act, he obtains many other things besides. When the jiva is dissolved in this state, he perceives inner sounds such as those emitted by the drum, the conch, the tabla, the vina, or a buzzing. Meditate on this most high state. One then becomes imperishable, immortal, like a second Kamadeva. O Sundari! One should remain unified.

A rain of parijata flowers then appears. And then, one is worshipped by the maidens who serve the nagas, as it was for

Hatakeshvara. I have thus stated the facts concerning the five perceived sounds that bestow liberation. Devi, the characteristics of the sphere of Kula have been revealed to you because of your devotion.

Devi, something even greater will now be communicated to you: the characteristics of obstacles. One must establish the nameless in one's heart. In the dvadashanta one visualizes a lotus with its flower made of jewels. This act is called anama and it has the nature of space while being included within five seals, which are of the same nature as consciousness. Then, using the seals, one must break the obstacles that blind us through implementing a discrimination between the five seals and the dvadashanta on the path of Shakti. After being joined with the devis and the yoginis, the adept remains in their presence and reigns over the Matrka chakra. The yoginis dissolve in the Khecari chakra and one can arouse them using the ultimate amrita. O Devi, unless one uses amrita, how would it be possible to be amrita! Amrita is the true Kula path.

Listen to the essence of Kamakala. Blossoming within sahaja, there dwells a tattva, which is a pure precious stone like a pearl or a firefly. This tattva is as bright as a star and flourishes in the navel center, emitting rays that are white, red, yellow, violet, and black. It is the cause of both creation and dissolution when it takes on the appearance of a being and when it melts into nothing as it is devoid of both Kula and Akula. Through constant practice, the adept can create a solar orb. One's own body is perceived; by concerted efforts one can create the supreme body, without any doubt. O Varanane! Creation and dissolution occur in an instant. At night, the adept should worship Devi. At the center of two sugar canes . . . within resides the Supreme Devi, the cause and creator of both the animate and the inanimate. Everything dissolves in her yoni nadi. In making use of this stable doctrine, one becomes attached to neither merit nor fault. Through discrimination, the adept can achieve the sixty-four-fold form. By making use of the sixty-four-fold injunction, he can know which calera (chakra) is the origin of the siddhis. Thanks to his knowledge of the nature of Kula, and by being established in the Kula, the master of the supreme tattva on the Kulayana path can arouse sexual ecstasy with the vajra reed. In taking one's leave from gurus, siddhas, and devatas, that which is white as the Moon should flow into the sea of milk. In half a moment or less, one arouses agitation and is liberated from fever, illness, and ailments."

❖ Patala Fifteen ❖

Devi says: "O Bhairava! By Your Grace, speak to me of the consequences of birth and of the method for producing divinity. Explain to me now the results of tapas. Speak to me about this knowledge. My ears have been fascinated by the revelations of Mahakaula. Speak to me now of the resplendent pinda that contains within its whole a great knowledge stationed in the heart. Speak to me of the Kula mountain, and of the characteristics of the body. Reveal to me how one can move about at will or by your grace, O Devadeva. I am asking for what has not been revealed to me before; please reveal each part separately. Reveal to me everything concerning the mode of meditation that generates steady balance. Previously, you made me happy. Now, I am asking you to unveil what has not yet been revealed. The millions of creatures located in the center of the oceans, how have you survived in the terrible destructive deluge where the animate and inanimate dwell that you have spoken about? O Natha! Speak to me of how you protected yourself."

Bhairava says: "O Mahajnani! This question, which you have not asked me before, is well put. My protection has an inner meaning that must be concealed. Visualize skulls at the tips of the fingernails. In a similar way, one should visualize them inside the center of the chakra of the bones. This Sahaja chakra is known to be a powerful vajra. A man becomes a vajra by practicing Vajra yoga. Above a marvelous chakra with one thousand koti petals, there is another lotus with seven thousand million petals and filaments. Being surrounded three times with milk inside this lotus, one must force one's body to bathe in this milk. Inside its pericarp dwells the ultimate tattva that resembles an Atasi flower. Within it there are lotuses of five petals, eight petals, and a very beautiful lotus of sixteen petals. In the sixteen-petal lotus, a triangle appears. O Varanane! On each of the sixteen petals there is a lotus of eight petals. Next, the adept must split the bindu by dividing up the sixteen letters unified with the breath. By this dividing up of the sixteen letters, one becomes established in the upper chakra. Devi, one must carry out this practice four times in succession, otherwise not at all. The atma will be visualized merged with this lotus. After having placed one's atma in the circle of lotus petals, it will be dissolved in the upper chakra. Devi, one immerses the mind in that as one would immerse an object in cow's milk. O Sulocana! Then one visualizes that the eight petals of the lotus crown the lower lotus, making the breathing chakra as radiant as the lower chakra. One's body is thus plunged into the previous chakra, which resembles the Full Moon. This has the result that the chakra of the bones is immersed in this place of stillness. After having immersed the whole Cosmos in this way, the adept sets in motion the practice of the three chakras. Parvati! We must immerse everything in the highest chakra. By dissolving everything in what is like a slender reed, one is thus liberated from old age and wrinkles, from fever and illness as one becomes imperishable and immortal.

O Lady of the Word! When this dissolution is achieved, at that moment there can be seen simultaneously inanimate and animate things and, in this way, we, You and I, establish ourselves inside the chakra. The greatness of this act means that the adept obtains sovereignty over the Three Worlds, over animate beings and inanimate objects. He simultaneously becomes the cause of both creation and dissolution, by achieving forever a state of balance with the chakra of the bones in a state of dissolution. Very Dear One! Using this method, the body, like a vajra, cannot be dissolved. My occult path, this secret hidden until now, has been set forth in various ways and one must conceal it carefully. This Kula Sadbhava has been revealed to you."

Devi says: "Bhairava! The siddhi yoginis, in their divine forms, play and reside in the middle of the Matrka. O Natha! This remains unknown to the undiscriminating, or even to gods and gandharvas, the celestial musicians. Speak to me of the three sacred temples of the mountain, as well as the lands where you reside. O Devesha, narrate for me your wanderings as a beggar; explain to me your celestial vision. Speak to me, O Lord Deva, of the knowledge concerning the highest meditation."

Bhairava says: "Bhadre! This is a pure request relating to the marvelous sphere of the siddhis. O Vishalakshi! How could anxiety persist if one knows this tale?

It is said that the three pithas are Shri Shaila, Shri Mahendra, and Kamakhya Pitha. I reside there, all three constituting different parts of the siddhis. O Kuleshvari! Those noble persons who meditate concentratedly on the void in these places have the darshan that You and I accord them. On the mountains of Shri Shaila and Mahendra is the whole body of siddhis relating to rajas. It is said that sadhaka women expert in yoga dwell at Kamakhya Pitha. If one unites one on one, one achieves the yogini siddhis with more consciousness, mind, ability to adopt various appearances, and anima, as well as the eight other siddhis. Everything one wants can be obtained here. What more can be said of its magnificence?

Bhadre! The meeting places have been explained to you as you asked. As well, the fivefold essence of the siddhis, a secret teaching, can be obtained in these places. This must never be revealed! I am the Parama Tattva. My Dear One! I am Bhairava. I am Shiva, Isha, Shri Kantha, and Rudra. O Devi! I am the Fisherman, I am the Lord of the Viras. O Mahadevi! I am Ananta, I am Rudra. O Kuleshvari, I dissolve the Cosmos, I am dissolution itself! I am creation, the cause of all that is animate and inanimate.

In the Kulagama, those very ones who resort to me will be saved as the injunction stipulates. Indestructible in the universe, I am described in hymns as Vishva Pada who gives rise to all the many variations and the play of creation. I played, I acted, or one was acting according to my own will. Devi! Because I have white feet, people implore me like Shveta Pada. In bestowing my favors, I am radiant like the charming Moon and like the color of gold I am imperishable. That's why people claim that I am Bhrnga Pada.

Very Dear One! Both suras and asuras pray to me. That's why I am famous under the name of Bhatta Pada. Since I grew based on my love for Shri, I was called Shri Kantha. O Mahadevi! Being known as Ruru Pada, I am Rudra. I am your Lord when you are Uma. Because of my splendor and in my capacity as Lord, I am known as Shri Natha within the circle of siddhas. When I was the avatar of knowledge and you were Kamarupi, I revealed the tattva 'He Who Has Six Faces.' In my unmanifest form I revealed the knowledge of Kulagama in Candradvipa. My Dear One! Because of that, Kula originated in me in the sphere of that which has not been manifested."

Devi says: "What is the Island of the Moon* that You and I went to? What astonished the devis in the fact of achieving desires in Kaula? What is the form called Vatuka? What are the letters of his mantra and what is his dhyana? O Bhairava, I want to hear about all these things."

Bhairava says: "O Gentle-voiced One! I am known as Natha. You are Iccha, Jnana, and Kriya Shakti. You are also known as

---

*[Candradvipa means "Island of the Moon" as well as being a place-name. —*Trans.*]

being Gauri, Mahakali, Lakshmi, and Shri. O Vishalakshi, you and I are avatars of all the shastras. When you and I were going to Candradvipa (the Island of the Moon), we were joined by Vatuka Karttikeya. Even though he was ignorant, I entrusted this Shastra to him. O Devi! The instruction given to Skanda was in vain: he stole the knowledge and threw it into the sea. Bhadre! So I went to the ocean and after having caught the fish that had swallowed the Shastra, I made an incision to open its stomach. After having recovered the books of knowledge from the fish's stomach, I hid them in a secret location. Once more, Kruddha adopted the appearance of a mouse and stole them in order to throw them into the ocean. Once again, they were gobbled up by a fish of immeasurable size! Furious, I made a Shakti net. I caught this fish, which was submerged in seven seas. However, this fish was as strong as I was. Because of his spiritual strength, he was difficult to vanquish even for the thirty-three gods. Giving up my position as a Brahmin, I became a fisherman and I caught the fish with my Shakti net. By making a gash to open him, the Kulagama was recovered once again. Even though I was a Brahmin, O Supreme One, I acted as a fisherman. Since the Brahmin rescued the knowledge from the stomach of the fish by killing it, he was known as Matsyaghna.* Because the Lord of the Brahmins acted as a fisherman, he became Kaivarta (the fisherman)."

Bhairava says: "Because this great thing—the treatise being revealed—was previously declared by spiritual power, it is said that Kaula was born from the sphere of Avyakta. It was offered to you and to 'He Who Has Six Faces,' to Vighnesa, to Nandina, to Mahakala, to Jaya, to Vijaya, and to the very powerful Hara Siddhi. Thus, Kaliki Yogini is famous everywhere. I obtained this

---

*[Matsyaghna means "killer of fish" in Sanskrit. —*Trans.*]

Akula by making a pilgrimage and, at the end of this kalpa or yuga, it has remained within me. It dwells in the heart of jiva, inseparable just as the fruit and flowers are inseparable from the roots of a plant, or just as the leaves and branches belong to a tree. O Kulabhamini! It resides in my body. Those who don't know about it are pashus. After having recovered this famous, grand knowledge for the second time, it was offered to you—to you, to Kameshi, to Skanda, to Gana, to Nandi, to Mahakali, to Jaya, to Vijaya, to Bhatta, to Dronaka, and finally to Hara Siddhika. The characteristics of Kaula were explained to a yogi by Kalika. From Mahakaula came the Siddha Kaula, and from the Siddha Kaula it was transmitted to Matsyendra. I have spoken of the avatars of the four yugas. During the first yuga, it was the Jnana Kaula, in the second Maha Kaula. During the third, it was known as the Siddhamrta and during the Kali Yuga, it was saved by me from the stomach of a fish. Devi, I have explained all that to you. It is called the Yogini Kaula in the present treatise: *Kaulajnananirnaya.*"

Devi says: "My Lord, the yoginis and the devis are enchanted by your words. Speak to me of the four Kula siddhas. Faint with happiness, each one holding a flower, they fall prostrate to the ground. Speak to me, My Lord! Explain the yoga practice concerning the nature of the Red Protector."

Bhairava says: "O Vishalakshi! You and I coupled in Candradvipa. 'He Who Has Six Faces,' Vatuka, and Ksetrapala were born from our union. As for Ksetrapala, he had seven kotis of knowledge. What is there that Vatuka does not know? O Varanane! He is like our son. Since he bestows siddhis to sadhakas in the very dark Kali Yuga, he is renowned in all the Tantras for his capacity to destroy curses. Now I'm going to speak to you about the practice that grants siddhis to a sadhaka with the bali, the pinda, and the asana mantras.

Hrim Vatukaya Kapilijataya Pingalanetraya Deviputraya Matrputraya Imam Balim Mamopanitam Grhna Grhna Curu Muru Hrim—this is the bali mantra. *Cala Cala Bhaksa*—this is the pinda mantra. The wise man should make offerings with that and he should then also offer the pinda. *Hrim Vatukaya*—this is the asana mantra. *Hyaum Hyauhyam Mahabhairava*—this is the puja mantra. One should recite the *Hrim* formulation. Whoever recites the following mantra clears all obstacles in his worship and siddhis are granted to him. One must say: *Grhna grhna*. Then Vatuka clears all the obstacles. One must meditate on Vatuka who is wearing red clothing, holding a staff, and has matted hair. He is as luminous as Brahma, the destroyer of obstacles.

Hrim Vatuka—one must recite this vidya when suffering from a great anxiety. There are many methods explained in the shastras connected to the siddhis of evil being. O Surasundari! Hrim is the mantra of Vatuka. A Kaula must worship him to obtain all the siddhis."

❧ Patala Seventeen ❧

Devi says: "My Lord. Speak to me about what I have asked you. What are the characteristics of atma? I want to hear about that. Please dispel my doubts."

Bhairava says: "And well you should ask, O Lady of the Yoginis and Siddhas. This great yoga stresses that the breath of life is stationed in the centers of the anus, of the genitals, of the navel, of the heart, of the lotus of the great uvula, of the ghantika wherein are the granthis and the 'great white place,' of the base of the nose at the dvadashanta, in-between the eyebrows, on the forehead, at the Brahmarandhra, and at the shikha. In this way, the eleven subtle centers are shown. They are known to reside in the body's central axis. Without having knowledge of this secret of Kulagama, men are afflicted. In the heart there resides Sahaja Deva, known as being the letters 'Ha Sa.' The letter 'Ha' is eternal, lacking any division. It is said that divisions are assigned to the letter 'Sa.' The syllable 'Sr' is always associated with creation, while 'Hi' destroys the Cosmos. 'Sa' is the bright fortnight and 'Ha' is the dark fortnight. 'Ha' is the visible form, while 'Hum Ha' is beyond all that. Just as fire and smoke cannot exist separately, Shiva cannot be without Shakti, just as Shakti cannot be separated from Shiva. Just as there is no tree without its shadow, nor shadow with its tree, in Kula practice one must understand that the yogi and his Shakti are inseparable. My Dear One! The gross, the subtle, and the supreme all reside in Hamsa. Knowing that, one is aware of the essence of being. In the Kaula parampara, this doctrine has been transmitted orally. It cannot be shown to someone who has not been tested, but only to those who have been. After initiating a person into Kula, one can reveal to him the characteristics of the essence of being. Deveshi, one must be aware of the five jewels of Kulagama. The first stops old age, the second gives whatever one desires, the third is Kamarupa, the fourth bestows immortality, and the fifth great jewel destroys fever and death. Seated on a cadaver in a house in a desolate place or nearby such a place, one must focus one's attention on the dvadashanta using perfume, incense, and beautiful flowers. After doing that, one should put on white clothing and draw a yantra with sandalwood paste. On this yantra, one must place a cushion and sit there accompanied by one's lover in a state of union with the Cosmos with one's senses withdrawn.

My Dear One, he who knows the ultimate circle of universality is unaware of either incense or foul smells, either camphor or sandalwood. In such a state, he is freed from time and can have a vision of the future. Devi, Mother of Heroes! In this state it is possible create and destroy, because Hamsa withdraws from the lower and the higher in order to be absorbed in the thousand-petalled lotus. This great balance is stationed in the heart just as water is contained in a pot. He is free to be or not be, all-knowing, without either meditation or the absence of meditation. He vibrates both above and below, even though he always remains himself. The Sahaja Tattva sexually plays like self and non-self.* The following sentence seems to refer to it. O Devi! In having become aware of this tattva, one frees oneself from being's attachments. In listening to the inner sound of the heart, one can know the qualities of Hamsa. In the throat chakra, this celestial sound, dhvani, has Kalas, the nature of which is cause and effect. Above the last underworld, it (Hamsa) is called Vama, having been wrapped from above and invested with form. From a point near the anus, it rises

---

*From the Magee translation.

up until it is absorbed once more in the dvadashanta. Thus, Hamsa moves around in the centers of the body, being neither good nor bad, stainless, lacking an organ, celestial, pure, very subtle, transparent, unified, eternal, blissful, giving birth yet free from birth. One must know that Hamsa is sexual force, the Natha, supreme, the essence of great knowledge, existence, the incommensurable, the incomprehensible, exhalation and inhalation, thought, absence of thought, moving in the four spheres of the elements, the atma, the Self, the Pinda, which can simultaneously create and destroy. O Sulocana! In this Pinda subject to unhappiness, happiness, slavery, despair, sleep, fever, death, hunger, thirst, illusion, fear, greed, poverty, and attachments, Hamsa cannot be cut to pieces by a sword or torn apart by a discus. It cannot be broken by vajra, burnt by fire, drowned in water, or even destroyed. It is not subject to illusion, attraction, desire, lust, greed, or anger. It is not fettered by anxiety. O You Who Bestow Favors! It is the essence of all the senses and the elements. This jiva, the Lord of Jivas, is at the origin of creation in the universe. It is soul, Hamsa, the Self, Shiva, emanation, cosmic mind. It exists in both the animate and the inanimate. Knowing that, one exists and one does not exist; one makes the gift of ecstasy and liberation simultaneously. One should first of all connect to one's guru, the very essence of Self. After being connected, the adept can access liberation because, of all beings, the guru expresses the essence of being. After having become aware of the Self of all selves, of the atma in its bodily form, he can liberate us on the yoga path. He is Shiva, it is said. Clearly, a being who is that liberated can liberate another being. O Devi! He is always pure, seated on a lotus. He is the Paramatma. Through his touch, one achieves the state of liberation—of that there can be no doubt. My Dear One! Instructed by him, one becomes free. By bathing him, the being becomes free. In bathing him, in anointing him, or in being sprinkled by water from his feet, one becomes joyous and liberated. In thanking this unified Being, the adept enjoys all things. He who bathes him gains merit of being bathed in all sacred water crossings. If his essence is discovered, the result in its totality is won. He is the essence of the true siddhi yogini, and of the hosts of the Viras and the Mothers. He is great goodness—he who bestows both liberation and joy."

⛤ Patala Eighteen ⛤

Devi says: "My Lord! State for me the complete knowledge concerning the Kula Island, the Siddhas, happiness and worship, and the steady atma that resides permanently in the body. What is Kama of the Kaula Siddhas? What is the meaning of abhiseka, the consecration?"

Bhairava says: "I will speak about the methods concerning Kula Dipa, as well as rice flour or wheat flour cakes, since you have asked me about them. Surasundari! After preparing a cake made of milk, saffron, and the finest ghee that is presented in a circle of twelve oil lamps, one uses the *Hrim* mantra to worship the siddhas, the yoginis, and the guru. The puja will be conducted two or three times this way and one must always worship them first. O You Beloved of the Yoginis! The most excellent bija *Hrim* must be recited next. The yoginis are certainly intimately linked to the Eternal Being who bestows liberation and joy. I am now going to present another method concerning abhiseka in the Kula sphere. One must pour rakta (blood), and shukra (sperm), in equal proportions, using one of kunda, gola, or udbhava mixed with wine and ghee. Rakta is the vamamrita. Mixed with wine and sperm, it is the Absolute itself. The liquor is fermented with a mixture of buk flowers and black flowers. Wine is the bliss of consciousness and the creator when prepared with devotion. One should recite the mantra of the guru, the siddhas, and the devatas: '*Hrim Klim Mhau Jum Sah.*' After having conducted the act of worship according to the given regulations, one will make use of a conch or a pot to worship the guide who has a strong will and knows the characteristics of All. Then one should bow while performing the Anjali mudra toward Jaya, Ausadhi, Mohana, and all the other divinities. O You Whose Womb Is Fertile! One will recite the mantra according to the rule. In the center reside the five jewels combined with blood, which is surrounded by the oceans of salt, of milk, of curd, of ghee, of wine, of sugarcane juice and water, the cause of birth. In the center of all of that are the eight Kula Mountains. On one's own head will be visualized the Veshya Kumarika and her instructor. Then he makes offerings to them. In doing this, the adept becomes a yogi. Once again, I'm going to speak to you about the puja, as you've asked me to do. Equal amounts of blood and sperm are offered. Jaya Devi is delighted by the fact that the method of union is being used. Also, the offerings will consist of brown rice, white rice, as well as other beautiful and magnificent substances. The act of worship is conducted with the sixty-four upacaras. O Beloved Mother! After having attained union with the Guru and gathered all the upacaras with the appropriate preparation, the yoginis of the Siddha Viras appear. From that point on, one makes the offering. Wine will be drunk and meat consumed. Then, one pours out as an oblation the ghee mixed with sugar—all that together poured into the pot one thousand times, one hundred times, sixty-four times, or eight times. After accomplishing the Vira sadhana, one should thank the devis again and again. He who is familiar with the rule should offer grain and he shouldn't do it sparingly. In making use of the remainder of the rakta on the yoni, one obtains siddhis. The rest of the rakta is to be placed as a general offering in the pot or the conch. The puja must be conducted in the order prescribed by the shastras. By using all the ritual accessories and thanks to the prescribed preparation, the adept can become a siddha yogi by using this method."

❧ Patala Nineteen ❧

Devi says: "O Deva! Speak to me now of the placement of the lotuses in the body of the siddhas."

Bhairava says: "All of Devi's limbs in the chakra are very radiant and have heavenly forms. In practicing, the adept finds himself in the center of these sixteen petals. When one is seeking liberation, one should meditate on the auspicious devis who are dressed in white. When one desires the presence of the siddhi yoginis, one should meditate on them as being black-skinned, young, maidenly, wearing red clothing, smeared with blood, wearing red ornaments, adorned with flowers and red garlands. Each one of them should be worshipped as united with oneself. When one wants something, one should meditate mentally on Shri Natha coupled with his yogini who is holding a conch and is surrounded by hosts of subtle forms."

✢ Patala Twenty ✢

Bhairava says: "Devi! Listen to the marvel that bestows liberation in this world. The Natha must squeeze the nectar in one's genitals, heart, and throat. What has fallen must be reestablished at a higher level using pranayama. In piercing one's skull, the jiva becomes indestructible. This jiva, after being diffused, is both creator and destroyer, O Varanana! The atma is the supreme Knower and the witness of both the moving and the fixed. This sattva devoid of characteristics knows neither happiness nor unhappiness. Devi! One must present offerings to this source of pure consciousness. He who progresses on the path of sexual love of Shakti must restrain his senses when taking food and when having sexual intercourse, so that the anama is squeezed above the navel and the heart. After settling oneself and one's vital breath in sama consciousness, one worships devi in a flower or through images. Paying homage in this way, after six months of practice, allows one to attain the highest state of balanced breathing and perfect detachment. Deveshi! After many years of being united with space and the void, one becomes able to take possession of another's body by means of worship. O Marvelous Lady of the Heroes! Listen now to what concerns the Kula Shakti of the Vira and to Shakti's characteristics. She is called Iccha Shakti because she originates from Shiva, the receptacle of that which is without origin. She is known as being Vyoma Malini and Khecari. Vama Shakti is called Kundalini, Jyestha, Manomani. She is the Rudra Shakti that one terms Kamakhya in the hymns. O Foremost of the Devis! In certain still secret writings she is Matrka, the aggregate of Shabda, famous in all books."

Devi says: "Jnana Shakti is known to me. My Lord! Speak now about Kriya Shakti."

Bhairava says: "Now I will explain the characteristics of the vira and his Shakti. She is the ultimate one with eyes of dazzling white. She is a devi with disheveled hair, very beautiful and eloquent, her ten arms radiating outward. She is devoted to Kula and worships the devi of the guru. She is beautiful, joyful, and has a perfect countenance with nice eyebrows. She devotes herself to the Kulagama, free of all fear, very calm, exquisitely fine in nature, expresses herself with truth, free from the slightest doubt. She knows nothing of cruelty. She is a devi with a perfect body, aware of her beautiful appearance like the heroine who is the Shakti of Rudra—the "Root Devata." He who, having learned of the origin and the location of the Maha Lingam, the stem of the flower in flames, can become like the bindu. The unalterable Shakti of all the Shaktis is the internal Shakti of the atma. After becoming aware of this Shakti who originates in one's body, one can unite with her. In this way, one attains both knowledge and discrimination, as well as a nature exempt from duality. Such are the characteristics of a devoted vira in the Kula Kaula Agama."

✣ Patala Twenty-One ✣

Devi says: "My Lord! Speak to me of various schools in the Kula sphere."

Bhairava says: "I will speak to you of the characteristics of the various schools. There are fifty-five doctrines connected with yoga. In the Kaula Shastra, one can discern various lesser and greater differences. Representative of these differences are the Kaula Panca Shikhamula, the Kula Sagara, the Kula Ogha, the Kula Hrdaya, the Bhairava Udyanka, the Candra Kaula, the Jnana Kaula. Also, within these schools are schools called Sambara, Srsti Kaula, Maha Kaula, Timira, Amirta Siddha, and Kula Kaula Mata. Then there are the Shakti Bheda Kaula, the great Urmi Kaula, and in the four yugas the Jnana Kaula. There are the Siddheshvaras, the Vajra Kaula, and the Kaula created by Megha long ago. At the time of the full moon or new moon, or on the eighth or fourteenth tithi (day), when the anga is touched, it would be good to make an offering to Vajra Amrita—an offering of oneself as well as fish, meats, and so forth. One is to sacrifice an animal, explaining and teaching without the slightest hesitation. Tirtha, naksastra, and fasting are useless. The Kaula pathways are thus listed in the Jnana Nirnaya."

✥ Patala Twenty-Two ✥

Devi says: "I bow to you using the Anjali mudra and I question you again O Hara, Lord of the Nature of Siddhis! The six faces of Mahakala are Kalika Yogini, Nandisha, Bhattaka, Dronaka, Vijaya, and Mahabhaga. These are the six yoginis who are the Mothers. O Bhairava! I am still in doubt about Kaulamrta. Reveal all to me."

Bhairava says: "The Kulagama that the devatas discussed in the Bhuloka and which formerly was hidden is now revealed. The remainder can be taught by a Kula Siddha. But one must distinguish it from ordinary dualistic paths. My Very Dear One! In the whole universe, the hidden lingam remains the primary thing, and what is superior to it is still the act of worship of the guru who is full of compassion toward jivas. After having heard the discourse of Bhairava, the skin of all the devatas was shot through with a discharge of happiness. Their minds being perfectly satisfied, they fell to the very ground like simple sticks.

Kula devotion is the supreme thing. The extensive tree of samsara has now been cut down and the veil of ignorance torn apart. All fetters, nets, delusions, and sad doubts have been dispelled. There are ten and a half million elements in the path leading to knowledge. Among them, the Natha way is the quintessential core. In Kamarupa, the present shastra about the yoginis is present in every home. Those possessing this knowledge, a knowledge bestowed by divine grace, make use of it tirelessly. They are able to either favor or punish since they are unified with the yoginis.

Sulocane! This great shastra has been revealed in Candradvipa. In Kamakhya, it is the hymn that arises from the depths of Mahamatsya."

❖ Patala Twenty-Three ❖

Devi says: "How do the Kaula yoginis move about on the Earth, O Deva?"

Bhairava says: "In the world of mortals, all the devatas can move around there. Hear me! They exist as female turtledoves, vultures, swans, and as hens and other birds; also as female dogs, wolves, owls, falcons, bees or beetles, jackals, sheep, buffalo, cats, camels, mongooses, tigers, timid elephants, peacocks, and cuckoos. In various other female forms, the yoginis can live on Earth. It is imperative to venerate these forms and the yoginis delight in them. Merciful Kuleshvari: When they die, they should not be eaten. They also exist as horses, cocks, snakes, stags, and some who appear as human beings or appear as scorpions, bulls, mice, or frogs. We can be perturbed by the planets, bhutas, flames, fires, swords, difficult situations, obstructions, disease, kings, lightning, tigers, lions, or elephants. Additionally, we can be under the influence of various anxieties, causing things to appear from any direction. In this case, we must seek the protection of the sixty-four yoginis who wander in various forms by taking on the appearance of various animals. We must never say or think anything arising from anger toward these forms. In the same way, we must never speak harshly to maidens or women. We worship women and maidens because they represent Shakti placed under Kula protection. They are worshipped with various flowers that are scarlet red such as pomegranate, parijata, champaka, kunda, kadamba, simhakesha, bhandhuka, jati, utpala, lotus and all the other flowers. One worships them with various other beautiful blossoms and garlands such flowers of the shala tree. Meditate on them by visualizing them dressed in red clothing, besmeared with red scented paste, and adorned with red garlands. A vira should always meditate on them and worship them inwardly, while avoiding all acts of exterior worship. O Merciful One! The puja bestowing joy and liberation has been explained to you."

Ꙩ Patala Twenty-Four Ꙩ

Devi says: "My Lord Bhairava! Show me your full compassion. O My Lord! Speak to me of suras and asuras, of the nature of Mahakaula, of Kulakaula and the great knowledge. Beings are wandering in the ignorance and hell of samsara. Destroy this noose and net of samsara! Speak to me of liberation and independence. Instruct me! This is difficult to know. Kaulesha, once again, speak of Siddha Puja in the body."

Bhairava says: "I will speak clearly of the Kaula Puja. Listen! The Kula siddhas, the yoginis, the Rudras, and the Devi chakra all dwell in the head and heart centers. My Dear One! Listen to the rules of the external puja. One offers a sweet perfume, camphor, garlands of beautiful flowers, champaka blossoms, sweet-scented blue lotuses, red blossoms, a diversity of one hundred different flowers, tree resins mixed with honey, meat tambula, soma, incense, sandalwood, aloe wood, musk, very red flowers, fragrant kinds of incense and flames. Flowers devoid of scent are terrible and should not be presented as offerings. The external puja has been explained. Listen now concerning the meditation. All the yoginis will be dressed in red and their faces will be coated with red paste. They must make up a group of sixteen having sweet faces and adorned with jewels. They will drink a liquor distilled from madira flowers. Like Iccha, each one of them is freed from fever and death. Each one of them will be the cause of creation and will grant her own favors. He who meditates on them will live long."

Conclusion

*J*f the text of Matsyendranath's *Kaulajnananirnaya Tantra* had not been miraculously recovered by Pradodh Chandra Bagchi in 1922, the preeminence of the yoginis in Kashmiri tantrism would have remained unknown. No other tantra provides as complete a range of these powerful and iconoclastic practices that the monks tried to suppress in order to minimize the influence of women in this mystic path.

In them, we find the entire wild splendor of these practices, which provide a direct and very physical understanding of the "cosmic body" and of union with "all that is." Here, the yogi is in direct contact with experience. There is no progression, stages to pass through, or secret practices. The whole is immediately conveyed, right up front. Mystical ecstasy is seen as the body being equated to infinite space.

The yoginis saw the master-disciple relationship as an intense heart-to-heart experience: no wasting of time, no prerequisite purification, and no milestones to get beyond. They considered that the powerful impact of their physical presence was enough to shatter our concepts, our convictions, and our beliefs in order to lead us to nakedness of being, to the presence of the divine within.

This is what this text reveals to us, imbued with the magic of a time freed of all religious conformism.

Glossary

adhara: the meditative foundation.

Agama: tradition.

ajapa: silence.

Akula: Shiva in his state of crazy wisdom.

amrita: sublime essence.

anga: body part.

anama: one who does not bow down to others, a Brahmin.

anima siddhi: the power to become very small.

anjana siddhi: the power of clear vision.

Antyaja: a low-born woman.

artha: purpose, essence of being.

asana: seated position.

asura: spirit, ghost, or demon.

asuri: feminine form of *asura*.

atma: the Self.

bali: ritual food offering.

Bhairava: the secret, terrible, nocturnal form of Shiva.

Bhairavi: mother goddess and consort to Bhairava.

bhuta: ghost or spirit.

bindu: the primordial droplet, the center.

bija: syllable.

bogha: pleasuring.

Brahmarandhra: the vital center, the seat of consciousness.

buddhi: intelligence, discernment.

chakra: wheel, energy center.

citta: reason, intelligence, the silent mind.

Dakini siddhi: the powers of the Dakini.

deva: a deity.

deva kanya: fluidity.

devata: one who makes offerings to the gods.

devi: the feminine form of *deva*.

dharma: teaching.

dhvani: celestial sound.

dhyana: meditation.

dvadashanta: the crown chakra.

gandharva: celestial or aquatic beings.

gandharvi: celestial musicians.

ghantika: a measurement of time in twenty-four minutes.

gola: a lunar or terrestrial globe.

granthi: a knot of energy.

Hamsa: the creative act and all objects of creation, the perpetual breath.

Iccha: desire.

Iccha Siddhi: the power to see the future.

jiva: filled with devotion.

jnana: knowledge.

kala: time, energy.

Kalagnirudra: the god of fire, Rudra, original form of Shiva, destroyer of darkness.

Kali Yuga: a period of chaos.

kalpa: a long period of time, an age.

kama: desire, love.

Kamakala: the supreme tattva.

Kaulika: an adept of Kaula.

Khadga: a ritual knife.

Khadga siddhi: sexual power.

Khecara: messenger of the gods, spirit of the air.

Khecari: the ether-Shakti.

kinnara: celestial spirits.

kinnari: the demigods.

koti: the highest number.

Kriya: action.

Kruddha: rage, violence.

Ksetraja: that which emerges from the yoni, born of a womb.

Kula: Shakti, community, spiritual family (also *Kaula*).

Kulagama: the Kaula Way.

Kulacara: the Kaula or left-hand path.

Kulaja: that which is born of the Kula.

Kulasadbhava: the name of a Kula tantra.

Kuleshvara: the male incarnation or idealized representations of the Kaula (or Kula) Way.

Kuleshvari: female form of *Kuleshvara*.

kunda: fragrant frankincense resin.

Kusu Malini siddhi: special powers.

laghiman: levitation.

Lakini siddhi: the powers of Lakini.

lingam: a phallic representation of Shiva.

mahasiddhas: a practitioner of the siddhi of perfection.

Matrka: the power of speech, also refers to the eight goddesses.

moksha: liberation.

Mrtyuinjaya: accumulation.

nada: sound.

nadi: subtle channel.

naga: mythic serpent.

Natha: tantric group in the tradition of Matsyendranath.

Paduka siddhi: the power to move at the speed of lightning.

parampara: an uninterrupted order.

pashu: animalistic limitations.

patala: chapter.

Patala siddhi: the exploration of subterranean worlds.

pinda: supreme consciousness.

pitha: seats of power.

pranayama: breath control.

puja: worship ritual.

Rajada: movement, energy.

Rakshasi siddhi: terrifying protective power.

rakta: blood.

rasa: any substance produced by the body in a state of bliss.

Rasa: orgasmic pleasuring and all alchemical knowledge (siddhi).

Raurava: the horror-filled hell of the Kali Yuga.

rishi: enlightened person.

Rocana siddhi: the power of satisfaction.

sadbhava: existence.

sadhaka: yogi.

sadhana: spiritual practice.

sahaja: spontaneous enlightenment.

salagrama: a fossilized shell representing Vishnu.

sama: equanimity.

samadhi: ultimate meditative consciousness.

samsara: cycle of death and rebirth without beginning or end.

sandoha: the exposition of principle.

sattva: luminosity, consciousness.

shakini: female deity, attendant of Shiva.

shastra: treatise.

shikha: flame, ray of light.

shukra: sperm.

siddha: one with the power of siddhis.

siddhi: magic powers.

soma: magic plant, ritual drink, sublime essence.

spanda: continuous vibration.

sura: demigods.

tabla: drum.

tantrika: one who follows the sadhana of tantra.

tapa: endurance, austerity.

tattva: a modality of reality.

Tridanda: trident, three points.

tika: red dot between the eyebrows.

tilaka: a colored point on the third eye chakra made with sandalwood.

tithi: day.

udbhava: creation of the material world.

unmani: no mind.

Upacara: the way, the approach.

upapitha: sacred place.

Uttistha siddhi: the power of stout-heartedness.

vajra: indestructible scepter.

Vama: left hand tantric practice.

vamamrita: wine.

veshya: courtesan class.

vina: stringed instrument.

vira: hero.

vidya: knowledge.

vidyadhara: one who holds worldly knowledge.

vikalpa: dream, illusion.

yaksha: nature spirit.

yakshi: the magic beings, the inhabitants of the abysses.

yantra: mystical diagram used in meditation.

yoga: spiritual practice.

yogini: female practitioner.

Yogini siddhi: the power of the yoginis.

yojana: measurement of distance.

yoni: womb and vulva, representation of Shakti.

yuga: era, age.

Index

Page numbers in *italics* refer to illustrations.

BOOKS OF RELATED INTEREST

Crazy Wisdom of the Yogini
Teachings of the Kashmiri Mahamudra Tradition
by Daniel Odier

Tantric Kali
Secret Practices and Rituals
by Daniel Odier

Tantric Quest
by Daniel Odier

Yoga Spandakarika
The Sacred Texts at the Origins of Tantra
by Daniel Odier

Desire
The Tantric Path to Awakening
by Daniel Odier

**Meditation Techniques of the Buddhist
and Taoist Masters**
by Daniel Odier

Shakti
Realm of the Divine Mother
by Vanamali

Kriya Yoga for Self-Discovery
Practices for Deep States of Meditation
*by Keith G. Lowenstein, M.D.
with Andrea J. Lett, M.A.*

INNER TRADITIONS • BEAR & COMPANY
P.O. Box 388 • Rochester, VT 05767
1-800-246-8648 • www.InnerTraditions.com

Or contact your local bookseller